P9-BTN-470
WITHDRAWN

SUPERMAN
NEW KRYPTON

VOLUME **FOUR**

JAMES ROBINSON & GREG RUCKA
<WRITERS>

PETE WOODS
(PARTS SIX TO TWELVE)
RON RANDALL
(PARTS EIGHT TO TWELVE)
<ARTISTS>

BRAD ANDERSON
NEI RUFFINO
PETE PANTAZIS
BLOND
<COLORISTS>

STEVE WANDS
<LETTERER>

WITHDRAWN

<SUPERMAN> **CREATED BY JERRY SIEGEL AND JOE SHUSTER**

Fitchburg Public Library
5530 Lacy Road
Fitchburg, WI 53711

//

MATT IDELSON <EDITOR-ORIGINAL SERIES>
WIL MOSS <ASSISTANT EDITOR-ORIGINAL SERIES>
BOB HARRAS <GROUP EDITOR-COLLECTED EDITIONS>
ROBBIN BROSTERMAN <DESIGN DIRECTOR-BOOKS>

DC COMICS
DIANE NELSON <PRESIDENT>
DAN DIDIO AND JIM LEE <CO-PUBLISHERS>
GEOFF JOHNS <CHIEF CREATIVE OFFICER>
PATRICK CALDON <EVP-FINANCE AND ADMINISTRATION>
JOHN ROOD <EVP-SALES, MARKETING AND BUSINESS DEVELOPMENT>
AMY GENKINS <SVP-BUSINESS AND LEGAL AFFAIRS>
STEVE ROTTERDAM <SVP-SALES AND MARKETING>
JOHN CUNNINGHAM <VP-MARKETING>
TERRI CUNNINGHAM <VP-MANAGING EDITOR>
ALISON GILL <VP-MANUFACTURING>
DAVID HYDE <VP-PUBLICITY>
SUE POHJA <VP-BOOK TRADE SALES>
ALYSSE SOLL <VP-ADVERTISING AND CUSTOM PUBLISHING>
BOB WAYNE <VP-SALES>
MARK CHIARELLO <ART DIRECTOR>

//

Cover by Gary Frank with Brad Anderson
Publication design by Robbie Biederman

SUPERMAN: NEW KRYPTON VOLUME 4
Published by DC Comics. Cover, text and compilation
Copyright © 2010 DC Comics. All Rights Reserved.

Originally published in single magazine form in
SUPERMAN: WORLD OF NEW KRYPTON 6-12. Copyright © 2009,
2010 DC Comics. All Rights Reserved. All characters,
their distinctive likenesses and related elements featured
in this publication are trademarks of DC Comics. The stories,
characters and incidents featured in this publication are entirely
fictional. DC Comics does not read or accept unsolicited
submissions of ideas, stories or artwork.

DC Comics, 1700 Broadway, New York, NY 10019
A Warner Bros. Entertainment Company
Printed by RR Donnelley, Salem, VA, USA
(4/29/11) First Printing.
ISBN: 978-1-4012-2775-3

SUSTAINABLE FORESTRY INITIATIVE
Certified Chain of Custody
Promoting Sustainable Forest Management
www.sfiprogram.org
Fiber used in this product line meets the sourcing requirements of the SFI program.
www.sfiprogram.org SGS-SFI/COC-US10/81072

WORLD OF NEW KRYPTON <PART SIX>
COVER ART BY **FERNANDO DAGNINO** AND **RÁUL FERNANDEZ** <WITH MAZI>

OH RAO...
SUPERMAN
KRYPTONIAN BY BIRTH, YET EARTH'S GREATEST HERO. AFTER THE RECENTLY RECOVERED POPULATION OF KANDOR CREATED A PLANET FOR THEMSELVES, SUPERMAN LEFT HIS ADOPTED HOMEWORLD AND RELOCATED TO NEW KRYPTON. HERE HE ISN'T THE HERO. HERE, WHERE EVERYONE HAS HIS POWERS, HE IS SIMPLY...
KAL-EL
--NO LONGER THE LAST SON OF KRYPTON.
MEDIC! WE NEED A MEDIC HERE--
ZOD! ZOD!

FOR MY PEOPLE!

THEY'RE TEARING HIM APART--

FOR KRYPTON.

--WASTE OF TIME AND RESOURCES, YOU ASK ME.
WE NEED TO QUESTION HIM.
WE NEED TO THROW HIM BACK TO THE MOB, EL! IN RAO'S NAME, WE KNOW HE DID IT, FOR WE ALL SAW HIM SHOOT THE GENERAL!
BUT WE DON'T KNOW WHY, GOR.
GENERAL ZOD IS THE HEAD OF THE MILITARY GUILD...
...THE MAN RESPONSIBLE FOR THE DEFENSE OF NEW KRYPTON.
IF I UNDERSTAND OUR CHAIN OF COMMAND CORRECTLY, LEADERSHIP FALLS TO THE NEXT IN LINE, THE COMMANDERS...
...YOU, ME, AND COMMANDER URSA.
NO, YOU'RE CORRECT, WE'RE IN CHARGE NOW.
WHICH MEANS DEFENSE IS NOW OUR RESPONSIBILITY.
IF THIS WAS PART OF SOMETHING ELSE, SOMETHING BIGGER...
YOU'VE MADE YOUR POINT.
I'LL HAVE HIM MOVED TO THE INTERROGATION SPHERE IMMEDIATELY, MEET YOU THERE.
COMMANDER?
...COMMANDER URSA...?
...I...
...I NEED TO BE WITH THE GENERAL.
OKAY, GOR...

"...LET'S GET SOME ANSWERS..."
CALIBRATION COMPLETE.
GENETIC SCANNING SEQUENCE COMPLETE.
SUSPECT IDENTIFIED: LANCEPESADE RAL-DAR, SON OF YSSEY AND SER-DAR.
BORN 34 B.B.*, IN THE CITY OF ERKOL.
INDUCTED: MILITARY GUILD, AGE 20. COMMISSIONED AS LANCEPESADE, SECOND GRADE, 3 B.B..
ASSIGNED TO UNIT: COBALT SKY. SPECIALIZATION: INFILTRATION AND INTELLIGENCE.
ALL READINGS NOMINAL.
BEGIN INTERROGATION.
* BEFORE BRAINIAC
YOUR NAME IS RAL-DAR.
THIS IS COMMANDER GOR, AND I'M COMMANDER KAL--
I KNOW WHO YOU ARE.
EVERYONE KNOWS WHO YOU ARE, KAL-EL.
LET'S NOT PLAY GAMES.

FINE BY ME, YOU PIECE OF DRANG EXCREMENT.
DID YOU REALLY THINK YOU WOULD GET AWAY WITH MURDERING ZOD?
I EXPECTED TO BE CAUGHT, IF THAT'S WHAT YOU'RE ASKING.
TRUTH.

WERE YOU ACTING ALONE?

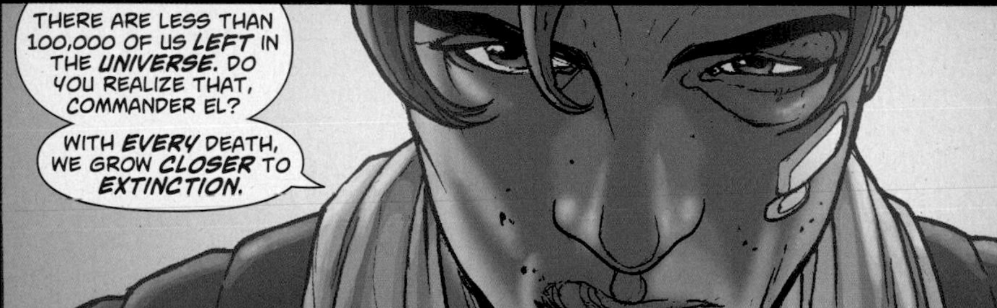
THERE ARE LESS THAN 100,000 OF US LEFT IN THE UNIVERSE. DO YOU REALIZE THAT, COMMANDER EL?
WITH EVERY DEATH, WE GROW CLOSER TO EXTINCTION.

SOMETHING HAD TO BE DONE TO ASSURE OUR SURVIVAL.
YOU HAVEN'T ANSWERED MY QUESTION.
I THINK I HAVE.
TRUTH.

WERE YOU ACTING ALONE? DAMMIT, WERE YOU?!?
EVERYTHING I HAVE DONE, I'VE DONE TO SAVE MY PEOPLE.

TRUTH.
TREASON IS PUNISHABLE BY DEATH, RAL-DAR.
YOU SAY YOU'RE TRYING TO SAVE US, BUT YOU'VE JUST MOVED US TWO LIVES CLOSER TO THE EXTINCTION YOU FEAR.
THAT DOESN'T MAKE SENSE.
THERE ARE ALWAYS SACRIFICES FOR SURVIVAL, COMMANDER.
I AM A MEMBER OF THE MILITARY GUILD, I HAVE TAKEN A HOLY OATH TO RAO AND ALL WHO ATTEND HIM TO DEFEND MY PEOPLE.
I WILL DO WHATEVER IS NECESSARY TO SEE US SURVIVE.
TRUTH.
THIS IS GETTING US NOWHERE
COMMANDER EL, I HAVE A MESSAGE FROM ALURA ZOR-EL...
...YOU'RE REQUIRED AT THE MEDICAL FACILITY IMMEDIATELY.
I'VE GOT TO GO.
PUT RAL-DAR BACK IN HIS CELL, COMMANDER GOR.
WE'LL CONTINUE WITH HIM WHEN I GET BACK.
WITH PLEASURE, COMMANDER EL...
...THE LESS I HAVE TO LOOK AT HIM, THE BETTER...

KAL!
HOW IS HE?
IT'S NOT GOOD, KAL. WHATEVER HE WAS SHOT WITH, IT'S DONE TREMENDOUS DAMAGE ON A CELLULAR LEVEL.
WE'RE STILL TRYING TO ARREST THE EFFECT, BUT NO MATTER WHAT WE DO, IT SEEMS ONLY TO AMPLIFY IT.
WE'VE HAD TO PUT HIM INTO STASIS TO PREVENT A CASCADING FAILURE.
DO WE KNOW WHAT HE WAS SHOT WITH?
THE WEAPON WAS SHATTERED WHEN THE ASSASSIN TRIED TO FLEE.
KARA GATHERED ALL THE PIECES SHE COULD FIND, BUT I HAVEN'T HAD A CHANCE TO EXAMINE THEM YET.
GENERAL ZOD REGAINED CONSCIOUSNESS JUST BEFORE WE HAD TO PUT HIM INTO STASIS, KAL. HE WAS IN INCREDIBLE PAIN.
HE ASKED FOR YOU.
FOR ME?
BUT WHY...?

MA'AM!!!

LYRA? WHAT IS IT?
MA'AM, YOU HAVE TO DO SOMETHING!
CALMLY, LYRA. EXPLAIN, PLEASE.
IT'S--ALL THE PEOPLE, THE ONES OUTSIDE, THERE'RE THOUSANDS OF THEM--
--THEY'RE SCARED, MA'AM, THEY THINK IT'S HAPPENING AGAIN, LIKE WITH BRAINIAC--
--THAT KILLING ZOD IS THE START OF AN ATTACK--
DEAR RAO...
I'LL SPEAK TO THEM, AUNT...
...SEE IF I CAN'T OFFER SOME REASSURANCE--
NO, KAL.
IT'S MY JOB.

--GOING TO DIE WE'RE ALL--
KANDOR, LISTEN TO ME!
--CAN'T DO IT AGAIN, I CAN'T, I JUST--
--KILL THE GENERAL? WHO WILL PROTECT US IF--
--THOSE GREEN LANTERNS, OR EARTH, MAYBE--
--HATE US, THEY ALL HATE US--
LISTEN.
WE ARE ALL WORRIED. WE ALL SHARE THE MEMORIES THAT THIS UNPROVOKED, VIOLENT ASSAULT ON OUR BELOVED GENERAL ZOD STIRS.
WE HAVE LOST SO MUCH. OUR WORLD, OUR FAMILIES, OUR FRIENDS AND LOVERS AND CHILDREN. WE HAVE BEEN PRISONERS. WE HAVE BEEN WITHOUT HOPE.
YET WE HAVE COME SO FAR! WE HAVE MADE A NEW HOME, WHERE WE ARE FREE!
WE HAVE MADE AN AIR TO BREATHE, HAVE ENCOURAGED NEW LIFE TO GROW!
WE HAVE SURVIVED. MORE, WE HAVE OVERCOME! WE HAVE BECOME STRONG!
REMEMBER THAT STRENGTH NOW, AND WITH IT, OUR COURAGE!
THE ACT OF ONE MAN ALONE IS NOT ENOUGH FOR US WHO HAVE ENDURED SO MUCH TO LOSE OUR FAITH!
ZOD STILL LIVES! BE AS HE WOULD HAVE US! HAVE COURAGE! HAVE FAITH!
AND BE NOT AFRAID.

NICELY DONE, ALURA.
MY HANDS WON'T STOP SHAKING.
I HATE SPEAKING IN PUBLIC.
TELL ME I HAVEN'T LIED TO THEM, KAL. TELL ME THIS ASSASSIN ACTED ALONE.
WE'RE STILL TRYING TO DETERMINE THAT.
THE COMPANION OF FEAR IS HATRED.
IF THIS ATTACK ORIGINATED FROM OFF NEW KRYPTON, I DON'T THINK I'LL BE ABLE TO KEEP OUR PEOPLE FROM DOING SOMETHING WE'LL ALL REGRET.
YOU'VE GOT TO FIND OUT THE TRUTH.
I'LL HEAD BACK THERE, NOW.
I'LL COME WITH YOU.
LYRA, GIVE THEM MY COM.
USE IT IF YOU NEED TO REACH ME IMMEDIATELY.

WHAT THE--
CHECK THE GUARDS!

UNCONSCIOUS.
MINE, TOO.
DID HE BREAK OUT, OR...

...WHAT'S THIS? LOOKS LIKE A SUNSTONE REPLICATOR...
NAR, IT'S EL.
SIR!
RAL-DAR HAS ESCAPED. ALERT ALL STATIONS, GENERAL QUARTERS.
TEAM TO MEET ME AT HOLDING 6, SECTION 2

IF THAT'S HOW HE BROKE OUT, AND IT WAS OUTSIDE OF THE CELL...?
YEAH.
I'VE SEEN THIS BEFORE.
COMMANDER!

GQ IS ON, SIR!
WE'VE SPOTTED RAL-DAR ON PLANET-WIDE.
THEY LOCKED ON HIM LEAVING THE ATMOSPHERE, SPACE-BOUND. TRAJECTORY PUTS HIM ON COURSE TO--
--EARTH?
YES, SIR.
WHEN HE SHOT ZOD--HE SAID "FOR KRYPTON!"
IF HE'S HEADED TO EARTH...
AND KARA...
...I'LL CATCH UP WITH YOU...
...I HAVE TO GET SOMETHING FIRST.

OKAY--KARA--
RED SHARD, LET'S GET OUR BOY. THERE'S NO PLACE ON NEW KRYPTON HE CAN HIDE.
HE'S NOT ON NEW KRYPTON, SIR!
YES. HE COULD START A WAR.
RED SHARD, STAND DOWN. THE LAST THING WE NEED ON EARTH IS A KRYPTONIAN MARTIAL UNIT SHOWING UP. KARA AND I WILL HANDLE THIS. ALONE.
NO, THE LAST THING WE NEED IS "COMMANDER KAL-EL" ON EARTH.

THIS IS A JOB FOR SUPERMAN

FOLLOW SUPERMAN'S PURSUIT OF GENERAL ZOD'S ASSASSIN IN THE *SUPERMAN: CODENAME: PATRIOT* COLLECTION.

WHEN SUPERMAN PURSUES RAL-DAR TO EARTH, HE DISCOVERS THAT IT WAS GENERAL SAM LANE — LOIS LANE'S FATHER, A MAN LONG THOUGHT DEAD, BUT WHO SECRETLY HEADS A BLACK OPS GOVERNMENT AGENCY CALLED PROJECT 7734 — WHO CONVINCED RAL-DAR THAT THE ONLY WAY TO PREVENT WAR WITH EARTH WAS TO ASSASSINATE GENERAL ZOD. IN REALITY, INSTIGATING A WAR BETWEEN EARTH AND NEW KRYPTON IS EXACTLY WHAT GENERAL LANE WANTS.

HE CONTINUES TO MANIPULATE RAL-DAR BY LEADING HIM TO BELIEVE THE PRESIDENT OF THE UNITED STATES INTENDS TO SIGN A TREATY AUTHORIZING A WAR AGAINST NEW KRYPTON. SUPERMAN RACES TO STOP RAL-DAR BEFORE HE CAN MURDER THE PRESIDENT, BUT LANE STOPS RAL-DAR FIRST, KILLING HIM WITH BLASTS OF KRYPTONITE. IT WAS ALL A SHOW ON LANE'S PART — NOW HE IS BACK IN THE PUBLIC EYE, SEEN AS THE HERO OF EARTH; AND KRYPTONIANS LOOK LIKE A DANGEROUS THREAT.

WHEN SUPERMAN LEAVES EARTH WITH RAL-DAR'S BODY, HE IS MORE DETERMINED THAN EVER TO PREVENT THE WAR GENERAL LANE INTENDS.

WORLD OF NEW KRYPTON <PART SEVEN>
COVER ART BY **GARY FRANK** AND **BRAD ANDERSON**

"WHAT WE ARE FACING NOW IS AN ALIEN THREAT...
"...A RACE THAT HAS MADE THEIR CONTEMPT AND HATRED FOR OUR KIND CRYSTAL CLEAR.
"THEY HAVE ATTACKED US ON OUR OWN SOIL. THEY HAVE SOUGHT TO KILL ONE OF OUR GREATEST LEADERS.
"THERE IS NO OTHER INTERPRETATION OF THIS ACTION THAN A PRELUDE TO WAR! THEY HAVE FORCED OUR HAND! THEY LEAVE US NO CHOICE!
"AND IF IT IS A WAR THEY WANT..."

...THEN I SAY WE GIVE IT TO THEM!
WITH GENERAL ZOD STILL IN STASIS FROM HIS WOUNDS, I HAVE ASSUMED COMMAND OF THE ARMIES OF NEW KRYPTON.
WE ARE READY, WE ARE WILLING, AND WE WILL GLADLY LAY DOWN OUR LIVES TO DEFEND OURSELVES FROM EARTH.
THE COUNCIL HAS ONLY TO SAY THE WORD...
...AND WE CAN ATTACK WITHIN THE HOUR!
COMMANDER GOR, YOU ARE PROPOSING A PATH OF MUTUAL DESTRUCTION!
ARE WE EVEN CERTAIN THE ATTEMPTED ASSASSINATION OF GENERAL ZOD WAS THE WORK OF THE HUMANS?
COUNCILOR QIN IS CORRECT.
THE MAN WHO SHOT GENERAL ZOD, RAL-DAR, WAS NOT ONLY KRYPTONIAN, BUT A MEMBER OF THE MILITARY GUILD...
...THE SAME AS YOU AND I, COMMANDER.
COUNCILOR EL RECONSTRUCTED THE WEAPON RAL-DAR USED, SHE DETERMINED IT WAS FROM EARTH!
A WEAPON THAT HAS NO PURPOSE BUT TO MURDER KRYPTONIANS!
HAVEN'T YOU REALIZED WHAT THIS MEANS?
AN EARTH WEAPON WAS IN THE HANDS OF AN ASSASSIN, HERE, ON NEW KRYPTON!
WE HAVE TRAITORS AMONG US, COUNCILORS --
I HAVE TO ASK...

...HOW MANY MORE OF OUR PEOPLE HAVE TO DIE BEFORE WE FIND A WAY TO LIVE IN PEACE WITH EARTH?
HOW MANY OF US WILL FALL IF WE GO TO WAR?

YOU STILL TALK AS IF THAT COSTUME OF YOURS MATTERS.
WE ALL HAVE YOUR POWERS! WE HAVE SUPERIOR TECHNOLOGY, SUPERIOR TRAINING--
YOUR ARROGANCE NEVER CEASES TO AMAZE ME, GOR.
YOU'RE TALKING ABOUT FIGHTING EARTH, FIGHTING HUMANITY AND ALL THAT ENTAILS, AS IF IT WERE A FOREGONE CONCLUSION.
COUNCILOR QIN WAS ALMOST RIGHT WHEN HE SAID "MUTUALLY ASSURED DESTRUCTION."
BUT THE DESTRUCTION THAT'S ASSURED IS ANYTHING BUT MUTUAL.
YOU'RE TALKING ABOUT GENOCIDE...
...EITHER FOR THEM OR FOR US.
HONORED COUNCILORS...WE ARE A DEAD RACE THAT'S BEEN GIVEN A REPRIEVE.
KANDOR IS THE RESURRECTION OF KRYPTON. THE CHANCE FOR US TO REGAIN WHAT WAS LOST WHEN OUR HOME WAS DESTROYED.
SO I MUST ASK A SECOND TIME...
...HOW MANY WILL HAVE TO DIE BEFORE WE CAN FIND A WAY TO LIVE IN PEACE WITH EARTH?

RAO KNOWS I DO NOT WANT WAR, COMMANDER EL.
BUT WE HAVE SEEN NO EVIDENCE THAT EARTH HAS ANY DESIRE FOR PEACE WITH US.
AND FRANKLY, COMMANDER GOR HAS RAISED A TERRIFYING POINT...
...THAT EVEN NOW THERE ARE SPIES AND SABOTEURS HIDING IN OUR MIDST.
I MUST AGREE WITH WREN-ZA, KAL-EL...
...MY RECONSTRUCTION OF RAL-DAR'S WEAPON, MY ANALYSIS OF ITS COMPOSITION AND CAPABILITIES, LEAVE NO DOUBT AS TO ITS ORIGIN.
THE GUN WAS MADE ON EARTH.
YES, SOME OF THEM FEAR US, AND YES, SOME ARE CERTAINLY ACTING AGAINST US, BUT A WAR WOULD CONDEMN ALL--
WE'RE TALKING ABOUT OUR SURVIVAL, BUT YOU WANT TO ARGUE THE LENGTH OF A SNAGRIFF'S WINGS!
THERE'S NO QUESTION TO BE ANSWERED HERE! TRAITORS AT HOME, ENEMIES OUTSIDE!
IN YUDA'S NAME, THEY TRIED TO MURDER THE GENERAL! THEY TRIED TO MURDER ZOD!
THAT IN ITSELF SHOULD MAKE EARTH'S INTENTIONS CLEAR!

SPEAKING AS THE MILITARY GUILD'S LEAD REPRESENTATIVE TO THE COUNCIL, THE TACTIC DOES SPEAK FOR ITSELF.
THE ATTEMPT ON ZOD DENIED NEW KRYPTON THE MAN WE DEPEND ON MOST TO DEFEND US.
ONLY IF THIS CONSPIRACY IS AS GRAND AS COMMANDER GOR BELIEVES!
WITH RAL-DAR DEAD, WE CAN NEVER KNOW HIS MOTIVE!
A DEATH CONVENIENTLY ORCHESTRATED BY THE HUMANS, PRESUMABLY!
GENTLEMEN--
A TYPICAL MILITARY GUILD RESPONSE--
YOU'D RATHER WE HID IN ONE OF YOUR LABS, BEHIND--
GENTLEMEN, THAT'S ENOUGH.
WE ARE THE INTERIM RULING COUNCIL OF NEW KRYPTON, NOT SQUABBLING LABOR GUILD AGITATORS.
WOULD THAT GENERAL ZOD WERE HERE TO GIVE US HIS COUNSEL.
HE IS.

WHAT LITTLE *KOF* OF HIM REMAINS, AT LEAST.
YOU'RE OUT OF UNIFORM, COMMANDER EL.
JUST GOT BACK FROM EARTH, GENERAL.
SO I'D HEARD.
WITH THE COUNCIL'S PERMISSION, I WOULD LIKE TO SPEAK.
BY ALL MEANS, GENERAL.

⁑KOF⁑
I HAVE TWO THINGS TO SAY.
THE MILITARY GUILD'S PRIMARY DUTY--AND THUS, MY PRIMARY DUTY--IS TO DEFEND THE ⁑KOF KOF⁑ THE LIVES OF NEW KRYPTON.
SOMETHING, I FEAR, THAT ONLY A HANDFUL OF US TRULY UNDERSTAND.
SOMETHING THAT, IN MY CURRENT COND...CONDITION, I ⁑KOF⁑ CANNOT DO.
FOR THAT REASON, UNTIL I CAN RETURN TO DUTY...
...I AM PROMOTING COMMANDER EL TO THE RANK OF GENERAL, TO ACT IN MY STEAD.
KAL-EL NOW COMMANDS THE ⁑KOF⁑ ARMIES OF KRYPTON...
...AND SE-SECOND, FOR OUR OWN SAKE, THERE MUST BE NO WAR WITH EARTH...
...NOT YET...
DOCTOR!

IT'S WHAT I WAS AFRAID OF, HE'S DECOMPENSATING.
WE'VE GOT TO GET HIM BACK INTO STASIS!
GENERAL...?
...GENERAL? YOUR ORDERS?

WHAT DO YOU THINK, SIR?
HONESTLY, LIEUTENANT NAR? IT MAKES ME MORE THAN A LITTLE UNCOMFORTABLE.
BUT IT'S A GREAT HONOR, SIR! YOUR FLAG, FLYING THE EMBLEM OF YOUR HOUSE, THE HOUSE OF EL!
THAT'S WHY IT MAKES ME UNCOMFORTABLE.
BY TRADITION, THE GENERAL LEADING THE MILITARY GUILD DESIGNS AND FLIES HIS OR HER OWN HOUSE FLAG.
THERE IS NO SHAME IN IT, GENERAL EL. IT'S OUR TRADITION.
I SHOULD GO, SIR.
PERHAPS YOU'LL HAVE BECOME MORE USED TO IT BY THE TIME I RETURN.
PERHAPS.
GOOD LUCK, LIEUTENANT. I'M COUNTING ON YOU TO KEEP GOR FROM ATTACKING ANY STRAY ASTEROIDS YOU MIGHT ENCOUNTER.
I'LL DO MY BEST, SIR.

SIR? YOU WANTED THE REVISED TRANSIT FOR OPERATION: CALLISTO?
THANK YOU, LIEUTENANT HIN.
THIS IS BETTER, BUT I'M STILL CONCERNED WITH THE BREAKOUT FROM THE JOVIAN GRAVITY WELL.
WE'RE MOVING A MOON, I DON'T WANT TO DISRUPT ANY MORE ORBITS THAN WE HAVE TO.
COUNCILOR QIN RAN THE MATH HIMSELF, SIR.
ANY VARIATIONS CAUSED BY THE TRANSIT WON'T RESULT IN A SIGNIFICANT DEVIATION FOR AT LEAST THREE BILLION YEARS.
GLAD TO HEAR IT. SINCE CREATING A MOON FOR OURSELVES WASN'T FEASIBLE, WE NEED THIS PLAN TO WORK IF WE'RE TO CREATE OCEANS. MAKE SURE GOR GETS THIS REVISED ROUTE.
HE'S STILL IN STASIS?
OVER A WEEK NOW. SINCE HE MADE NON AND I BRING HIM BEFORE THE COUNCIL.
SINCE HE PROMOTED YOU.
EVERYTHING'S UNDER CONTROL HERE, COMMANDER URSA.
YOU'RE DISMISSED, IF YOU WANT TO HEAD OVER TO THE HOSPITAL.
...YES, SIR.

KAL...
...YOU SUMMONED ME.
DO YOU REMEMBER THE FIRST TIME WE MET, TYR? HOW WE SAW THE CITY TOGETHER.
YES, KAL. YOU WERE NEW AND SO WAS KRYPTON.
NOW THE PLANET BLOSSOMS AND GROWS WITH MORE LIFE EACH DAY.
AND YOU'RE ZOD'S REPLACEMENT. LOOKING AT HOW YOU WERE THEN, IT'S AMAZING WHAT'S HAPPENED.
WELL FIRST, I'M ONLY ZOD'S TEMPORARY REPLACEMENT.
BUT IN THAT ROLE, TYR, I'M STUCK WONDERING WHAT I SHOULD DO ABOUT SOMETHING.
OH?
MAYBE YOU CAN HELP ME WITH THIS, OKAY, PAL?
ER... I'LL TRY. I MEAN--I'M NOT--I'LL TRY.

SO HERE'S MY DILEMMA.
I HAVE THIS FRIEND. HIS NAME IS TYR-VAN. HE'S BEEN MY PAL SINCE MY FIRST OFFICIAL DAY AS A CITIZEN OF KRYPTON.
AND HONESTLY, IT'S BEEN NICE TO HAVE SOMEONE I COULD TALK TO.
SOMEONE I COULD TRUST.
BUT THEN I GOT INTO TROUBLE WITH ZOD. TROUBLE SO BIG I WAS GOING TO BE EXECUTED.
MY PAL TYR OFFERS ME THE MEANS TO ESCAPE...
...BUT I DECLINE. I DECIDE TO FACE MY FATE.
ZOD SURPRISES ME LATER--GETS MY "CRIME" PARDONED.
ZOD AND I LEAVE THE COUNCIL CHAMBERS TOGETHER
--AND THAT'S WHEN HE SLIPS UP. HE TELLS ME HE SEES NOW THAT I'M WILLING TO DIE FOR KRYPTON.
WELL, YOU WERE FACING EXECUTION.
A PERSON IS ONLY "WILLING" TO BE EXECUTED IF HE HAS THE MEANS NOT TO BE AND ELECTS TO DIE ANYWAY.
IF HE'S GIVEN A CHOICE.
SO, MY PROBLEM-- HOW DID ZOD KNOW I'D BEEN GIVEN A CHOICE, UNLESS MY FRIEND TYR HAD BEEN DIRECTED TO OFFER ME THE CHANCE OF ESCAPE BY ZOD HIMSELF?
I THOUGHT I HAD A FRIEND IN YOU, TYR--

--AND NOW I SEE YOU WERE ALWAYS JUST A SPY.
NO! I SWEAR! I'M NOT!
I'VE HAD A LIFETIME TO HONE MY POWERS, TYR, SO I KNOW WHAT A PERSON'S HEARTBEAT SOUNDS LIKE WHEN THEY'RE LYING.
I'M LABOR GUILD, KAL. I DO WHAT I'M TOLD.
I DON'T WANT TO SEE YOU ANYMORE.
BUT--
LABOR GUILD, RIGHT? THAT'S YOUR EXCUSE?
THEN DO AS YOU'RE TOLD AND GO!

COMMANDER!
OPERATION: CALLISTO WAS GOING PERFECTLY. THEY'D DISENGAGED THE MOON FROM JUPITER'S ORBIT AND WERE WELL ON THE WAY TO GETTING IT BACK HERE.
WE HAD MYN-GAI, ONE OF GOR'S LANCEPESADES, ON VISUAL. SHE NOTICED "SOMETHING" CRESTING INTO VIEW FROM AROUND MARS, BUT BEFORE SHE COULD SAY WHAT, WE LOST VISUAL AND NEARLY ALL AUDIO, TOO--
--SOME KIND OF JAMMER, WE THINK.
YOU SAID "NEARLY" ALL AUDIO.
YOUR LIEUTENANT NAR, SIR--
--HER COMMUNICATOR STILL WORKS-- BARELY.
THEY CAME FROM--
--TOO MANY--
--OSSIBLE FATALITIES--
--UNDER ATTACK--
--MMANDER GOR WAS IN THE EXPLOS--
RAO! THEIR GUNS ARE--
--MORE FROM EVERYW--
AHHHH--!
WHAT SHOULD WE DO?
WHAT DO YOU THINK?

RED SHARD.
BLUE STRIKE.
GOLD LASH.
SIR!
"LET'S GO!"

THERE'S MARS, SIR.
YEAH, KIR-TA, I SEE.
BUT WHAT I DON'T SEE ANY SIGN OF, YET, IS--

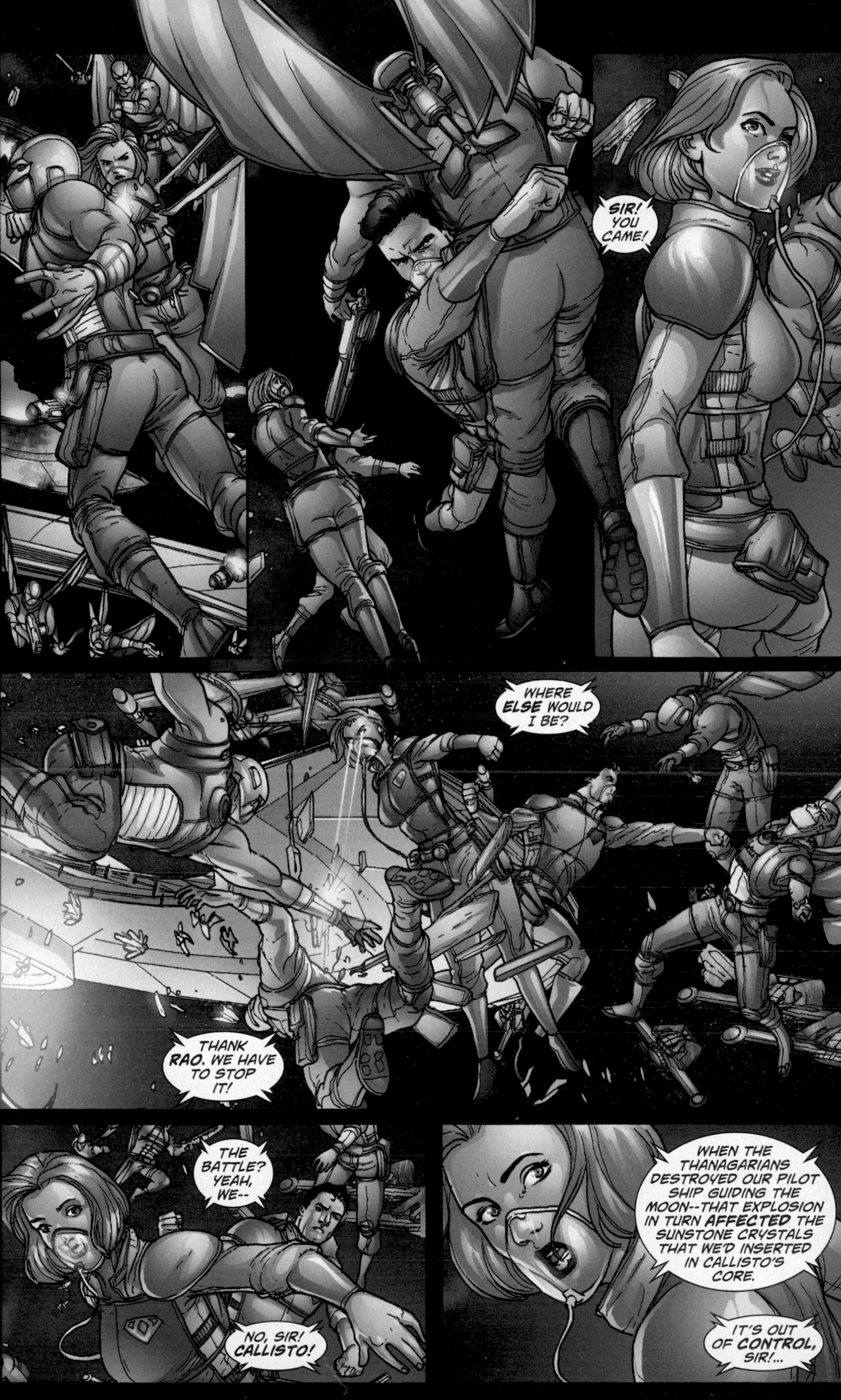
SIR! YOU CAME!
WHERE ELSE WOULD I BE?
THANK RAO. WE HAVE TO STOP IT!
THE BATTLE? YEAH, WE--
NO, SIR! CALLISTO!
WHEN THE THANAGARIANS DESTROYED OUR PILOT SHIP GUIDING THE MOON--THAT EXPLOSION IN TURN AFFECTED THE SUNSTONE CRYSTALS THAT WE'D INSERTED IN CALLISTO'S CORE.
IT'S OUT OF CONTROL, SIR!...

"...AND HEADING STRAIGHT FOR KRYPTON!"

WORLD OF NEW KRYPTON <PART EIGHT>
COVER ART BY **GARY FRANK** WITH **BRAD ANDERSON**

DEPLOY WINGMEN FLIGHT OSPREY TO BATTLE-SITE QUADRANT CINQO.
JAMMY MEAT!
FIGHT! FLASH!
FLASH THOSE KRYPTONIANS HARD--

--WE'LL CRACK THEIR DANWARD FLANK--
SEND THEM TO CELAE!
ONWARD TO--
REPORT STATUS OTHER SHIPS.

SEVEN DEVILS!
SHOOT! DON'T LET THEM--
IRBLE!
GRYFALCON TREI HAS 20% DAMAGE, WING-MASTER DAE. AIR LOCKS HOLDING.
THEY'RE DEAD AND THAT'S FLAT!

BY FAENEAR, I'LL KILL EVERY LAST--
KILL THIS WORTHLESS MEAT!
NO QUARTER FOR TH--

LOOK STRIKEWARD, TWERL! INCOMING Ks ON THE--
JAM! THANK BESKA OUR BLASTERS CAN--
FIRE UP--
BULWAR!

TOO MANY VOICES, NUL.
MAKE IT SO THAT THE ONLY ONE HEARD IS MINE.
AS YOU SAY, WING-MASTER DAE. AUDIO DOWN. BRIDGE HANDS SILENT EXCEPT NEED-TO-SPEAKS.

AH. GOOD. GRAND. TRANQUILITY AND BATTLE. NOW, VICE-WING NUL...
...WHAT IS OUR STATUS?
AFTER THE KRYPTONIANS ATTACKED US...
...OUR COUNTERATTACK CRIPPLED THE LEAD SHIP OF THEIR FLEET, WHICH WAS THE PRIMARY CONTROLLING VESSEL IN FERRYING THE JOVIAN MOON CALLISTO OUT FROM ITS ORBIT AND TOWARDS THE KRYPTONIANS' PLANET.
THIS TRANSPORTATION HAPPENING AT A SUPER-FAST RATE DUE TO THEIR SCIENCE...A SCIENCE THAT IS NOW WORKING AGAINST THEM AS THE BATTLE OUTSIDE UNFOLDS.
THOUGH WHY THEY WOULD WANT ONE OF JUPITER'S MOONS IN THE FIRST PLACE IS A RIDDLE FOR WHICH I SEE NO ANSWER.
WELL, YOU CAN SOLVE IT, IF INDEED SUCH THINKING IS WORTH THE EFFORT, ONCE WE'VE SHOWN THESE MEAT THE FACE OF SHEKKEL.
WING-MASTER! OSPREY UNIT UPPER QUADRANT IS FALLING BACK!
COMMUNICATE TO THEM THAT THEIR FAILURE HERE WILL MEAN SUMMARY EXECUTION FOR ANY SURVIVORS UPON RETURN TO THANAGAR.

WITH THE LEAD SHIP GONE, SO IS THEIR CONTROL OF CALLISTO. THE ORB IS NOW ON A RUNAWAY TRAJECTORY TOWARDS THIS "NEW" KRYPTON OF THEIRS, WITH NO APPARENT MEANS OF STOPPING IT.
TELL THE WINGMEN ELITE IN LOWER QUADRANT QUARTO TO PUSH ON.
WING-MASTER.
HELMSMAN.
OUR OWN GRYFALCON...

"...IT'S ENTERING A HOTZONE."
A STRIKE ON US!
WHAT DAMAGE SUSTAINED, NUL?
SOUND THE ORDER TO ABANDON SHIP, ALL FORCES TO CONTINUE FIGHTING WHEN JAMMIED THE VESSEL.
ORDER SOUNDED, WING-MASTER. LET'S JAMMIE TOO.
THIS IS MY SHIP--
YOU CAN GO.
I STAY.

GOOD.
GRAND.
THEN LET'S MAKE IT HOTTER STILL.
I WAS GETTING BORED ANYWAY.
ALL ABLE WINGMEN--
--TO THE GUNS!
SALVOS IN FOUR-TIME, MULTIPLE ROUNDS--
LET'S SHOW THESE KRYPTONIAN MEAT WE'LL TAKE NONE OF THEIR BULWAR.
ANGLE AROUND THEM--

ABACI REPORT FROM ENGINE LEVEL. THE REACTOR IS CASCADING.
STOPPER?
BEYOND THAT. BEYOND HOPE.
FLAT. ABACI SAYS WE HAVE BUT MOMENTS.

NO. WITH ALL DUE RESPECT, IF YOU INTEND TO SEE THE SEVEN HELLS--
--THEN LET IT BE A VIEW WE SHARE.

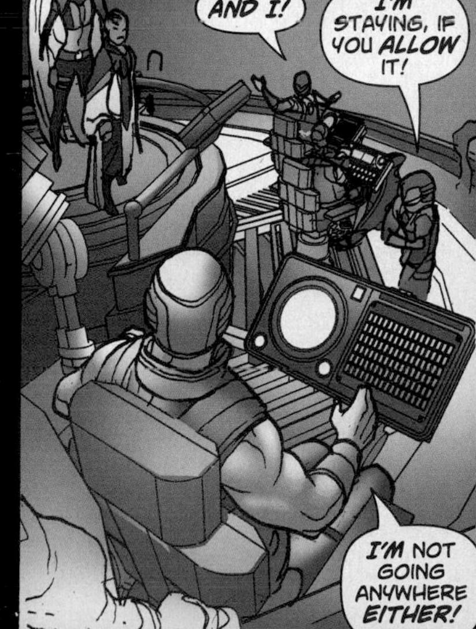
AND I!
I'M STAYING, IF YOU ALLOW IT!
I'M NOT GOING ANYWHERE EITHER!

AH, HERE COME THE KRYPTONIANS TO FINISH THE JOB.
THEY'VE BREACHED US, WING-MASTER, LARBOARD HULL.
ENGINE ROOM ABACI SENSORS CITE THEIR PRESENCE SHIP-WITHIN.
GOOD.
GRAND.
MAY THE BLAST TAKE A FEW OF THEM WITH US.
ER, WING-MASTER DAE-- ABOUT THAT BLAST OF WHICH YOU SPEAK--
--WE SHOULD BE DEAD BY NOW.
ABACI REPORTS--
--THEY REGISTER-- UM--THE CORE IS ON COOL-DOWN.

HOW?
I HAVE NO EXPLANATION. WE WERE TWO SECONDS FROM A RED LINE, IT ALL WENT COLD.
ABACI SCAN FULL RESET ACROSS THE CORE. REACTOR NOMINAL.
ENGINE ROOM! KEF--
WING-MASTER--
--BY ALL HELL'S DEVILS, WHAT--
--YOU NEED TO COME DOWN HERE RIGHT AWAY....

--SHIP FULL OF TWERLS, PUT THEM ALL ON...
...REPORT....

ENGINEER KEF, AN EXPLANATION.
NOW.
THE STRIKE FUSED THE COOLANT DUCTS, WE WENT STRAIGHT INTO RED-LINE...
...THE KRYPTONIANS MADE BREACH...
...AND THEN THEY SAVED THE SHIP.
GOOD.
GRAND...
...BUT A REMARKABLY FOOLISH THING TO DO FOR YOUR ENEMY, KRYPTONIAN.
IF YOU HAVE A NAME, I WOULD HEAR IT.
COMMANDER--
GENERAL.
--GENERAL EL. THIS IS LIEUTENANT NAR.
AND WHO DO I HAVE THE HONOR OF ADDRESS-ING?
I AM WING-MASTER VETALLA DAE, COMMANDING THIS BATTLE GROUP.
AT REST.
THEY ARE NOT PRISONERS.

YOU WOULD HAVE WON HAD YOU LET US DIE, GENERAL.
TO NO END.
NEW KRYPTON BEARS NO HOSTILITY TO THANAGAR, OR ITS PEOPLE.
BULWAR. YOUR PEOPLE STARTED THIS ACTION, GENERAL.
YOU DEMONSTRATE THIS LACK IN A STRANGE FASHION.
WING-MASTER, WHATEVER THE CAUSE OF THIS ALTERCATION, YOU HAVE MY WORD AS THE LEADER OF THE MILITARY FORCES OF NEW KRYPTON, IT WAS NEVER INTENDED.
I HAVE ORDERED ALL KRYPTONIAN FORCES TO IMMEDIATELY WITHDRAW.
YOU WOULD DO ME THE HONOR OF ALLOWING MYSELF AND MY PEOPLE TO NOW DO THE SAME...
...AS WE HAVE A MORE URGENT SITUATION WE MUST DEAL WITH.
VERIFY HIS WORDS.
...FLAT. ALL KRYPTONIANS HAVE WITHDRAWN.
GO.

NUL...
...THE JOVIAN MOON, HOW LONG BEFORE IT IMPACTS THEIR WORLD?
MY BEST ESTIMATE WOULD BE SEVENTY-THREE MINUTES, WING-MASTER.
HOW IS IT THEY CAN MOVE A MOON SO QUICKLY?
IT'S BRILLIANT, IF I MAY SAY SO, WING-MASTER, AT LEAST FROM THE LITTLE I WAS ABLE TO GATHER DURING THE BATTLE.
YOU SEE, THE KRYPTONIANS USED THEIR CRYSTAL TECHNOLOGY TO CREATE ANCHOR POINTS ENVELOPING THE SATELLITE, ESSENTIALLY CREATING A NEAR-RELATIVISTIC BUBBLE AROUND IT...
...THEN THE PILOT VESSEL CLAPS ON AND GUIDES IT THROUGH SPACE-TIME.
THEIR OWN FAULT, THEN. THEY SHOULDN'T HAVE UNDERTAKEN SOMETHING SO DELICATE WITH SUCH HASTE.
FLAT, WING-MASTER, IT IS NOT THEIR FAULT...
...WE DESTROYED THE PILOT SHIP IN OUR INITIAL STRIKE.
WITHOUT IT, THEY HAVE NO CONTROL OVER THE JOVIAN SATELLITE'S TRAJECTORY OR ACCELERATION.

GOR?
WE'VE BEEN TRYING TO SMASH THE SUNSTONE CRYSTALS CONTROLLING CALLISTO'S SPEED--
--BUT WE CAN'T BREAK THE ENVELOPE, AND WE'VE BEEN UNABLE TO LINK UP TO THE REPLACEMENT PILOT VESSEL.
SO NO WAY TO SLOW IT DOWN, LET ALONE STOP IT?
DAMN THANAGARIANS-- THEY MADE THIS HAPPEN. WE SHOULD--
LET'S WORRY ABOUT WHO EXACTLY DID WHAT, COMMANDER GOR, WHEN WE DON'T HAVE A MOON HURTLING TOWARDS OUR HOME-WORLD. WHAT DO YOU SAY?
ALL WE HAVE GOING FOR US IS OUR OWN BRUTE STRENGTH, AGAINST--
RAO KNOWS HOW MUCH SPEED AND G-FORCE WE'RE UP AGAINST.
ONLY ONE WAY TO FIND OUT, COMMANDER--
EVERYONE!
TOGETHER!

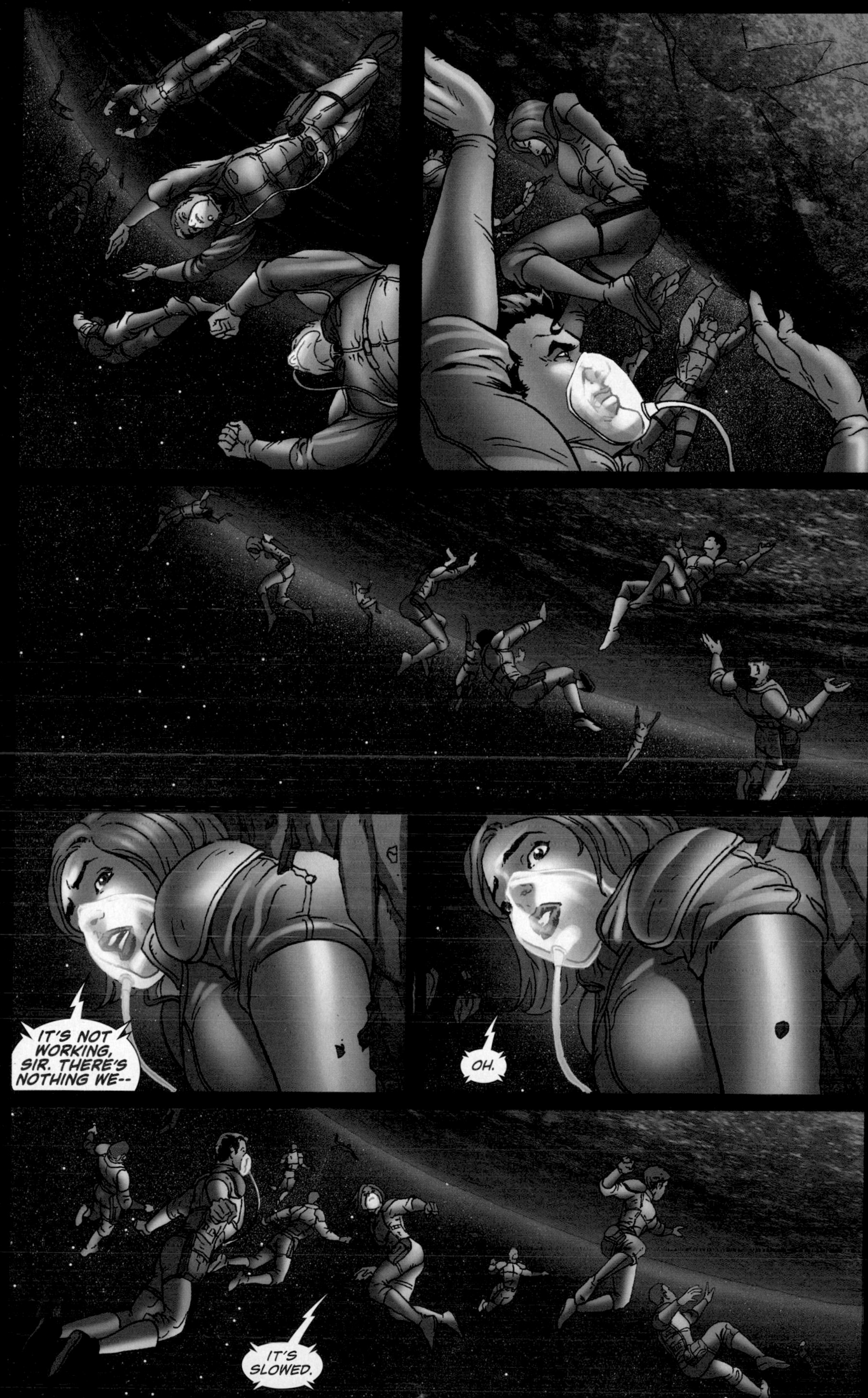
IT'S NOT WORKING, SIR. THERE'S NOTHING WE--
OH.
IT'S SLOWED.

DAE.
BUT-- HOW ARE THEY DOING IT?
NTH METAL... THEY MUST HAVE SOME MEANS TO FOCUS THAT ENERGY THROUGH THOSE BEAMS...

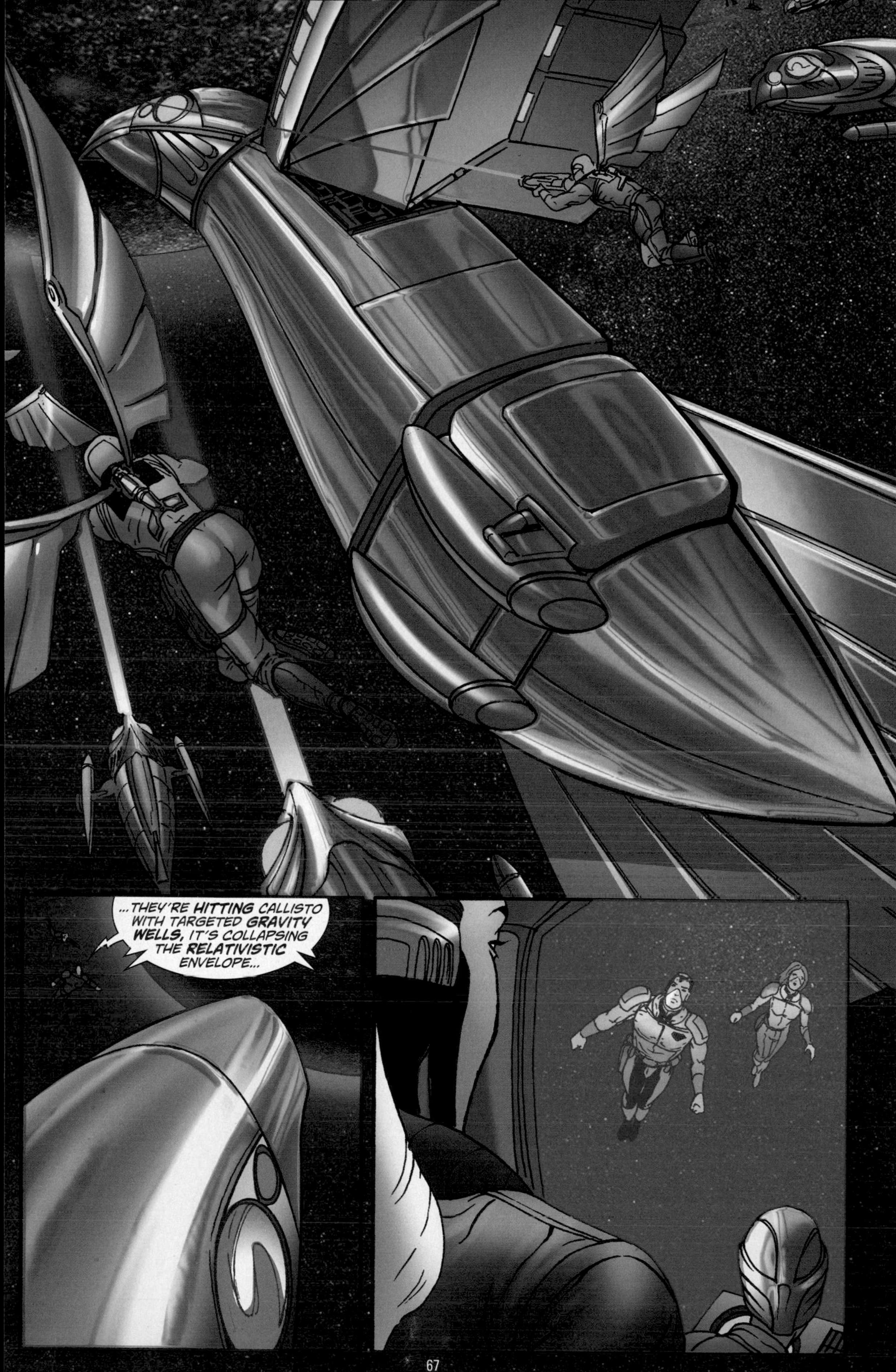
...THEY'RE HITTING CALLISTO WITH TARGETED GRAVITY WELLS, IT'S COLLAPSING THE RELATIVISTIC ENVELOPE...

MAIN BATTERY NOW DEPLETED!
DUO REPORTS THEIR EMITTERS HAVE GONE DEAD--
SPEED?
POINT ZERO-NINE, DE-CELERATING.
WING-MASTER...
...WE RISK THE BATTLE GROUP IF WE CONTINUE.
WE'VE DONE EVERYTHING WE CAN.
WE HAVE DONE OUR HONOR, VICE-WING NUL.
THE REST IS THEIRS TO RESOLVE.

SIR. IT HAS SLOWED DOWN, BUT IT'S--
--STILL ON A COLLISION COURSE WITH NEW KRYPTON, I KNOW. WE NEED TO ARREST IT--GET IT INTO PRECISE ORBIT.
WE COULD PUT MORE SUNSTONE CRYSTALS INSIDE IT.
YEAH, THAT WORKED SO WELL THE FIRST TIME, COMMANDER?
NO, IF WE PUT THE MOON INTO ANOTHER BUBBLE, IT COULD VERY WELL BREAK IT APART.
THEN WE'D HAVE METEORS BOMBARDING NEW KRYPTON INSTEAD.
WE NEED A NEW POWER SOURCE TO CONTROL IT'S GUIDANCE. SOMETHING TO--
WAIT! CALLISTO WILL BE KRYPTON'S MOON, RIGHT? THE MOON OF EVERYONE ON OUR PLANET.
YES, WHEN YOU PUT IT THAT WAY, SIR, THAT'S HOW I'D LIKE TO THINK OF IT.
WAIT HERE. I'LL BE BACK SOON.

"I RAN THE MATH AGAIN, MODIFYING OUR ORIGINAL CALCULATIONS..."
...EVEN WITH THE ADDITIONAL DISRUPTION CAUSED BY THE THANAGARIAN NTH ENERGY FIELD, THE GRAVITATIONAL EFFECTS OF CALLISTO'S TRANSIT ARE NEGLIGIBLE.
MEANING?
IN FOUR BILLION YEARS, MARS WILL COLLIDE WITH EARTH, AND NEW KRYPTON WILL PLUNGE INTO THIS SYSTEM'S SUN.
SINCE THE SUN WILL HAVE BLOOMED TO A RED GIANT AND ALL LIFE IN THIS SYSTEM WILL HAVE ENDED BY THEN, I FEEL REASONABLY SAFE.
YOU'VE STILL NO IDEA HOW THE CONFLICT WITH THE THANAGARIANS STARTED?
OH, I'VE GOT A VERY GOOD IDEA HOW IT STARTED, AUNT ALURA.
JUST NO PROOF AS YET.
AND THIS WING-MASTER DAE, SHE SEEMS CONTENT WITH THAT?
SHE DOESN'T TRUST US. THEN AGAIN, GIVEN WHAT HAPPENED, I WOULDN'T EITHER.
BUT THE DIPLOMATIC REQUEST IS SINCERE.
THEN THE COUNCIL WILL BE DELIGHTED TO HONOR IT.

...BEEN DIRECTED BY MY GOVERNMENT TO OPEN DIPLOMATIC CHANNELS BETWEEN THE PEOPLE OF NEW KRYPTON AND THANAGAR.
I CONFESS THAT THEY HAVE SOME RESERVATIONS.
KRYPTON IS A WORLD AND AN EMPIRE WELL-REMEMBERED BY MY PEOPLE, COUNCILORS.
WE WOULD BE FRIENDS.
TIME WILL TELL.
THEN SPEAKING FOR THE COUNCIL, I WOULD ASK THAT YOU TAKE YOUR LEADERS THIS MESSAGE:
WE ARE A NEW KRYPTON, AND WELCOME NEW FRIENDSHIPS. WHILE WE CAN NEVER FORGET THE SINS OF OUR PAST, WE ARE RESOLVED NEVER TO REPEAT THEM.
WITH THIS IN MIND, WE EXTEND TO YOU EVERY DIPLOMATIC COURTESY--
COURTESY?
COURTESY?!?
YOU BLUNDER AROUND THIS SYSTEM AS IF YOU OWN IT--

--BUT OTHERS WERE HERE FIRST.
I AM JEMM, AND I SPEAK FOR MY PEOPLE, AND ON THEIR BEHALF I ASK YOU--
--WHERE IS YOUR COURTESY NOW?

WORLD OF NEW KRYPTON <PART NINE>
COVER ART BY **GARY FRANK** WITH **BRAD ANDERSON**

COUNCIL SECURITY! WE HAVE INTRUDERS--
CHAMBER GUARDS ARE DOWN--
WHO ARE YOU?
YES, AND HOW DARE YOU INVADE THE SANCTITY OF NEW KRYPTON'S HIGH COUNCIL CHAMBER?!
WAIT! I KNOW HIM!
SO DO I! HIM AND HIS WHOLE DAMN RACE--
I JUST TOLD YOU, MY NAME IS JEMM. I AM A SON OF SATURN...

...AND I *WILL* BE HEARD!
FLANK AROUND-- ONLY A FEW OF THEM!
WE CAN TAKE THEM EASY IF--
EASY?

EASY?!

OH, THIS DAY WILL BE FAR FROM EASY!
YEAH, GUNS GET FIRED...

...AND THINGS GET SERIOUS.
GIMME THOSE!
DAE, HELP ME STOP THIS!

AS YOU SAY, GENERAL...
BUT IF IT WAS ME ALONE, I'D SHOW THESE SATURNIAN SCUM THE FIRE OF THANAGAR.
...I MAY LOOK DIFFERENT, BUT I'M SUPERMAN. REMEMBER ME?
YOU'RE THE RULER OF SATURN, I GET THAT. THE LEADER. BUT AS THAT LEADER, YOU SHOULD KNOW...
...THIS ISN'T A TIME TO FIGHT, JEMM.
THIS ISN'T THE TIME.

JEMM...
PERHAPS YOU ARE RIGHT.

NO, I THINK IN LIGHT OF THIS OUTRAGEOUS DISPLAY, WE, THE COUNCIL OF NEW KRYPTON, SHOULD VOTE IF WE'RE WILLING TO LISTEN TO THIS SATURNIAN AT ALL--
YOU POMPOUS IDIOT!
DO YOU THINK I NEED PERMISSION TO SPEAK?
ARE YOU SO SMUG AND STUPID, "NOBLE COUNCIL," THAT AFTER WHAT YOU JUST WITNESSED, YOU STILL FAIL TO SEE...
...THAT THE SATURNIAN RACE IS YOUR EQUAL?!
JEMM. STEADY.
AND YOU!
YOUR SMILE SUGGESTS YOU DOUBT MY WORDS.
I SMILE, BUT I AM SILENT, FOR IT'S NOT MY PLACE TO SPEAK.
NEW KRYPTON, I'M AGHAST AT THE ARROGANCE AND FEELING OF ENTITLEMENT, THAT YOUR PLANET CAN APPEAR AS IF OUT OF NOWHERE, AND ALMOST IMMEDIATELY BEGIN REARRANGING THE SOLAR SYSTEM.
YOU'RE BOLD TODAY, SATURNIAN, BUT I DOUBT YOU'VE DARED TO FACE EARTH IN THIS WAY.
...THAT I HAVEN'T ALREADY UNLEASHED THE FULL FURY OF SATURN UPON YOU.

BUT
I SENSE
YOU'D HAVE
PLENTY TO
SAY, IF--

KOKH. IF WE WERE ON
THANAGAR NOW, I'D DO
MORE THAN SPEAK,
FLAT.
YOUR PEOPLE
SIDED WITH THE RANNIAN
MEAT AGAINST US IN
OUR RECENT WAR.

AND HAVING
SEEN US UPON THE
BATTLEFIELD, DO YOU
THINK ANY LESS OF
MY PEOPLE'S MIGHT?

OH, I RECOGNIZE
EARTH'S VAIN FOLLY.
THEY ALSO ASSUME
THEY'RE THE ONLY
RACE WITH THE RIGHT
TO ABIDE IN AN ORBIT
AROUND THE SUN...
...A SUN WE
ALL SHARE.

BUT THEY'VE YET TO START MOVING
PLANETS AND MOONS AROUND TO
SUIT THEIR OWN NEEDS LIKE PLAYING
PIECES ON A ZUDANNE BOARD.

FOR WHAT YOU
DID, THANK GENERAL
EL HERE, AS YOU CALL
HIM--SUPERMAN AS I KNEW
HIM THEN. IT'S ONLY BECAUSE
OF HIS NOBLE ACTIONS IN
THE PAST, AIDING ME AT
A TIME WHEN I
NEEDED IT...

BUT YOU'RE
ON NOTICE, "OH,
GREAT AND MIGHTY
COUNCIL." WE WILL
BE WATCHING.

IN LEAVING, THOUGH...
...I ACKNOWLEDGE THE WONDER OF RAO.
FOR LIKE HIROMEER AND LOZORIL, YOU ARE A REAL AND MOST MAJESTIC GOD.

SO WE HAVE A PEACE.
NO, WE'VE AN ACCORD. THAT IS AS MUCH AS THANAGAR HAS EVER CEDED TO ANOTHER PLANET.
BUT AS THE SATURNIAN SAID...
...WE WILL BE WATCHING.

FOR SOMEONE CALLED THE VOICE OF RAO--
--YOU'RE AWFULLY QUIET.
NOTHING TO SAY?
THE VOICE SPEAKS WHEN RAO SPEAKS, GENERAL...
...AND RAO HAS BEEN SILENT TO US FOR A LONG TIME NOW, IT SEEMS.
COUNCILOR BIN-SE.
WE'VE GONE INTO RECESS FOR THE MOMENT.
IF YOU'D LIKE TO JOIN US?

--YOU TALK OF WAR AS IF LIVES WERE CHEAP, AS IF WE CAN AFFORD TO LOSE A SINGLE MAN OR WOMAN!
MILITARY GUILD BLUSTER THAT'LL GET US ALL KILLED!
ONLY AN ARTISTS GUILD FOOL MISTAKES PEACE FOR SUBMISSION!
GENTLEMEN--
OR HAVEN'T YOU NOTICED THAT OUR LIST OF ENEMIES GROWS EVERY DAY--
--EARTHERS, THANAGARIANS, AND NOW THIS KEKEL FROM SATURN--
KAY, CALM DOWN--
--THEY'D KILL US ALL IF THEY COULD, AND YOU WOULD PUT THE KNIVES IN THEIR HANDS!
NOT AGAIN.
HAPPENS A LOT?
DAILY.
GENERAL EL!
GENERAL EL! PLEASE, TALK SENSE TO YOUR COLLEAGUE!
COUNCILOR KAY-ZO IS RIGHT, WE ARE SURROUNDED BY ENEMIES.
CAN WE DEFEND OURSELVES, IF NEED BE? YES, ABSOLUTELY.
I THINK THE BETTER QUESTION IS, HOW CAN WE TURN THEM INTO FRIENDS?
WE DON'T NEED FRIENDS, GENERAL. WE NEED TIME.
NO OFFENSE TO YOU...

GENERAL'S MAKING HIS ROUNDS AGAIN.
WHY WOULD TODAY BE ANY DIFFERENT, KIR? THE ENTOURAGE WITH HIM?
GOR AND URSA...

...AND NON, THERE WE GO...

...HE FOLLOWS GENERAL EL AROUND LIKE SOME LOVESICK SNAGRIFF.

HOW ZOD COULD RATTLE URSA WITHOUT GOING CRACKED, RAO KNOWS.
NOT THAT I BLAME HER. EL'S EASY ENOUGH ON THE EYES.
YOU KNOW WHAT THE MONKEYS CALL HIM?

MAYBE SHE JUST WANTS TO SEE HOW SUPER HE REALLY...

YOU ALL SEEM TO HAVE FORGOTTEN THAT MY HEARING IS JUST AS SHARP AS YOURS.
AND SO IS THE GENERAL'S.

AFTER ALL HE'S DONE SINCE JOINING US, YOU STILL CUT PIECES OFF HIM BEHIND HIS BACK?

BEEN DOING IT FOR WEEKS NOW.
HE'S NOT THE ONLY ONE WHO'S LOVESICK.
COME-- RATCH!--AGAIN, JEQ?
NAR, YOU DULLARD...

...HAVEN'T YOU NOTICED SHE SPENDS EVERY WAKING HOUR IN EL'S COMPANY?
HISTORY, SHALL WE SAY, REPEATS ITSELF.

...IS...
...MA'AM.
RED SHARD! FALL IN!

BY THE FLAMEBIRD, YOU'RE RED SHARD! YOU'RE THE GENERAL'S OWN UNIT!
IF YOU DON'T RESPECT HIM, FINE--

--BUT HAVE SOME RESPECT FOR YOURSELVES!

MILITARY TRAINING QUADRANT
SO TO SUM UP COMMANDER GOR'S LESSON, EVERYONE...
...THERE'S ALWAYS SOMEONE STRONGER THAN YOU.

...ANOTHER SIX DOWN WITH THE SHAKES...
...BRINGS THE NUMBER TO SEVENTEEN THIS WEEK ALONE.
ALL OF THEM WORKING THE FARM DETAILS?
NO, IT'S SPREADING. SOME OF THE SCORCHERS IN ASSEMBLY RHO CAME DOWN WITH IT YESTERDAY.
IT'S NOT JUST AN ILLNESS, TAM-OR, IT'S AN EPIDEMIC.
WHY DOESN'T THE SCIENCE GUILD DO SOMETHING ABOUT IT?
YOU KNOW WHY. WE'RE LABOR GUILD.
WE'RE BENEATH THEIR NOTICE.
TYR-VAN'S RIGHT, TAM. WE WERE PROMISED A SEAT ON THE COUNCIL!
ALURA ZOR-EL GAVE YOU HER WORD!
UNTIL WE HAVE THAT SEAT, WE'LL NEVER HAVE ANYONE TO SPEAK FOR US.
TYR, PERHAPS YOU COULD ASK GENERAL EL TO PUT IN A WORD ON OUR BEHALF?
YOU ARE FRIENDS WITH HIM.
I WAS.

GENERAL ZOD...
...YOU'RE LOOKING BETTER TODAY.
YOUR EYES, I FEAR, DECEIVE YOU, KAL-EL.
MY RECOVERY IS A SLOW ONE.
YOU ASKED TO TALK TO ME?
YES. PREFERABLY ALONE.
NON, IF YOU WANT TO WAIT WITH URSA?
Nhn.

IS HE WORRIED I'LL ATTACK YOU?
YOU THINK ≷HNN≷ HE STAYS CLOSE TO YOUR SIDE OUT OF LOYALTY TO ME, KAL-EL?
SOME ≷HNN≷ IMPLICIT THREAT?
IT HAD CROSSED MY MIND, YES, GENERAL.
YOU COULD NOT BE MORE MISTAKEN.
YOU ARE THE VERY IMAGE OF YOUR FATHER.
HE SEES IN YOU HIS CLOSEST FRIEND.
THEN THE OLD COUNCIL STOLE HIS MIND AWAY.
HE LOOKS AT YOU, AND SOME PIECE OF HIM REMEMBERS WHAT HE WAS.
SO, TELL ME: ARE WE READY TO GO TO WAR?
DID YOU HAVE AN ENEMY IN MIND, GENERAL?
OR JUST THE UNIVERSE AS A WHOLE?

STILL SO SUSPICIOUS.
IT'S A QUESTION I WOULD ASK ANY MEMBER OF THE MILITARY GUILD, KAL-EL. PARTICULARLY THE MAN WHO LEADS IT IN MY ABSENCE.
I WOULD SAY WE STAND READY TO DEFEND NEW KRYPTON.
IF NEED BE.
JUST LIKE YOU TO CHANGE THE FIELD TO ONE MORE TO YOUR LIKING. A GOOD TRAIT FOR A LEADER OF SOLDIERS.
I'LL TAKE YOUR ANSWER AS A "YES," THEN.
TAKE IT AS YOU LIKE. THERE'S BEEN TOO MUCH TALK OF WAR IN THE LAST MONTH, GENERAL ZOD...
...I DON'T CARE FOR IT, AND I SEE NO NEED FOR IT--
GENERAL!
YES?
SOMETHING'S WRONG IN THE HIGH SECTOR...

"...AT COUNCILOR MAR-LI'S RESIDENCE...
"...HIS SUNSTONE METAFACE IS CALLING FOR AID."
WHAT'S HAPPENED?
READING ONE LIFE FORM INSIDE, DISTORTED, CAN'T FIX--
NO IDEA, GENERAL. THERE'S SOME SORT OF BAFFLE RUNNING, WE CAN'T SEE OR HEAR ANYTHING INSIDE--
--AND THE SECURITY SYSTEM'S BEEN TRIPPED, SEALING THE ROOM FROM THE INSIDE.
YEAH, NOT FOR LONG--
KRAK
THEN WE'LL DO IT THE OLD-FASHIONED WAY--

--GREAT RAO--
--ADAM STRANGE?!?

WORLD OF NEW KRYPTON <PART TEN>
COVER ART BY **GARY FRANK** WITH **BRAD ANDERSON**

RAO, HE'S KILLED--!
COUNCILOR MAR-LI IS DEAD!
KILL HIM!
WHOA, WHOA, WHOA. I DIDN'T--
ADAM? ADAM STRANGE? WHAT ARE YOU DOING HERE?

WAIT, YOU KNOW THIS ASSASSIN?
THIS IS ADAM STRANGE, KNOWN AS "THE MAN OF TWO WORLDS."
YES, WELL NEITHER OF THOSE WORLDS IS NEW KRYPTON, SO THAT MAKES HIM A SPY.
HOLD ON, GOR--
KAL-EL? THE MAN STANDS INSIDE A SEALED ROOM LOCKED FROM THE INSIDE.
THE ESTEEMED COUNCIL MEMBER MAR-LI LIES MURDERED BEFORE HIM.
SILENCE, MURDERER! HE IS GENERAL EL.
THANKS. NOW I KNOW HOW TO SILENTLY ADDRESS HIM. IDIOT.
AH, SOMETHING YOU DON'T WANT US TO SEE, PERHAPS?
NO, YOU BUFFOON...
...THIS IS A CRIME SCENE. LET ME REMIND YOU THAT THING ON THE FLOOR YOU'RE ALL TRIPPING OVER IS A DEAD MAN. ANYTHING...EVERYTHING HERE IS A POTENTIAL CLUE TO THE KILLER'S IDENTITY.
HE'S RIGHT. GOR, EVERYONE...OUTSIDE. NOW.
NAR. RED SHARD.
SIR?
SECURE THE ROOM. GET ALURA'S SCIENTISTS TO SCAN THIS PLACE.

FOR WHAT DO WE WAIT? WHY?
WE WAIT, COMMANDER GOR, BECAUSE UNTIL THE TIME THAT I AM RELIEVED OF MY RESPONSIBILITIES BY GENERAL ZOD...
...I AM YOUR SUPERIOR OFFICER AND I SAY SO.
I DIDN'T KILL THIS MAN, SUPERMAN.
STAND DOWN...ER... NAME?
LANCEPE-SADE VOL, SIR.
YEAH, WELL KEEP THOSE ANGRY THOUGHTS AND HEAT VISION IN YOUR HEAD.
DON'T TOUCH THAT!
SCAN? FOR WHAT, SIR?
OH MY GOD!
THIS ISN'T EARTH, ADAM. THIS IS THE FIRST MURDER ON OUR NEW PLANET.
AND MORE SO...

"...IT'S NEW KRYPTON'S FIRST MYSTERY."
SO YOU'RE SAYING IT WAS LUCK?
...ZETA BEAMS, WHILE BEING AN INCREDIBLE INVENTION AND MEANS OF TRANSPORTATION BETWEEN WORLDS, HAS NEVER BEEN AN EXACT SCIENCE.
YOU APPEAR SOMEWHERE, THE FIRST THING YOU DO IS LOOK AROUND AND THINK, "OKAY, I'M HERE, BUT WHERE THE HELL IS 'HERE' EXACTLY?"
ANYWAY... I ZETAED HERE...LOOKED AROUND...
...DEAD GUY ON THE FLOOR.

BAD LUCK. DUMB LUCK. BUT YEAH...
THE BEAM HAS A PROPERTY WITHIN IT THAT STOPS YOU FROM TELEPORTING INTO SOLID MATTER, SURE--
--BUT GOD HELP YOU IF YOU APPEAR SOMEWHERE FIFTY FEET IN THE AIR OR OVER AN OCEAN AND YOU'RE NOT WEARING A JET PACK.
BUT WHY COME TO NEW KRYPTON AT ALL?
I'M HERE TO DELIVER A FORMAL PROTEST.

INDEED? FOR WHAT?
YEAH, YOU'VE EVEN LOST ME ON THIS ONE, ADAM. PROTEST?
YOUR CHARTER WITH THANAGAR.
RANN JUST FOUGHT A WAR WITH THOSE MONSTERS...
...A WAR THAT WE LOST, ALONG WITH OUR WHOLE PLANET.
IT'S AN ANALOGY TO ONE OF EARTH'S DARKER PERIODS IN HISTORY.
WHAT DOES HE MEAN?
AND IT'S SOMETHING THAT BEARS FURTHER CONSIDERATION...
...BUT FOR NOW, IT DOESN'T HELP US SOLVE THIS MYSTERY AT HAND.
ADAM STRANGE IS FREE TO GO.

HE'S RIGHT. RANN IS GONE!
YEAH. LUCKILY...AND I USE THAT WORD LOOSELY...THE PEOPLE OF RANN HAVE A NEW HOME.

THAT PLANET IS NOW NEW RANN AS YOURS IS NEW KRYPTON.

THE THANAGARIANS ARE MURDERING, CONQUEST-HUNGRY THUGS WHO BELIEVE IN NOTHING BUT EXPANDING THEIR EMPIRE!
SIDE WITH THEM, YOU MAY AS WELL BE GOOSE-STEPPING INTO POLAND!

GENERAL EL! YOU EXCEED YOUR POWER!

LOOK, UNCOVERING A KILLER USUALLY BOILS DOWN TO THREE FACTORS...METHOD, MEANS AND MOTIVE.

MEANS...AS IN, COULD ADAM HAVE DONE IT? WELL YES, I GUESS SO. I MEAN... HE WAS IN THE ROOM.

BUT WITH THE IMPERFECT NATURE OF ZETA BEAMS, LET'S BUY HIS EXPLANATION AS TO HOW HE GOT THERE FOR THE MOMENT.

METHOD? SOME WEAPON THAT HARNESSED THE RED SUN...FOR NOW, THAT'S ALL WE KNOW.

A WEAPON YET TO BE FOUND. IT WASN'T ADAM'S PISTOL, WHICH, BY THE WAY, HAD NOT BEEN FIRED RECENTLY. IN FACT, THE "MYSTERY" WEAPON WASN'T IN THE ROOM AT ALL.

MOTIVE? NONE.

YEAH, I DON'T... DIDN'T KNOW THE DEAD MAN.

STRANGE IS OF EARTH. THERE IS MUCH TO BE GOTTEN FROM A COUNCIL MEMBER'S DEATH.

ADAM IS MORE OF RANN THAN EARTH. HE MIGHT NOT ADMIT THAT, BUT--

AND HIS REASON FOR BEING HERE DOES HAVE THE RING OF TRUTH.

I'LL TELL YOU WHAT, NOBLE COUNCIL, LET HIM HAVE HIS FREEDOM ON ONE CONDITION.

ADAM STRANGE IS KNOWN AS A SOLVER OF PROBLEMS. IF HE PROVES HIS INNOCENCE BY AIDING IN GETTING TO THE HEART OF THIS MYSTERY, HE CAN GO ON HIS WAY.

CONDITIONS, SUPES? COME ON, YOU HAVEN'T CHANGED THAT MUCH... YOU KNOW I'M INNOCENT.
CUT ME SOME SLACK, ADAM, YOU'RE DEALING WITH A CULTURE THAT'S WAY MORE DIFFERENT FROM EARTH...OR EVEN RANN.
I GOT YOU FREE, DIDN'T I?
YEAH, IF I PLAY BY YOUR RULES.
YEAH, WELL I ADMIT I MAY HAVE HAD THAT IDEA FOR SELFISH REASONS, BUDDY.
I'M NOT BRUCE OR RALPH. I REALLY NEED YOUR HELP ON THIS ONE.
MAYBE. BUT I HAVE A WIFE, DAUGHTER AND MEGALOMANIACAL TEAMMATE THAT I NEED TO GET BACK TO.
ADAM...
SIGH
WHERE TO FIRST?

THE CRIME SCENE. WHAT DO YOU SEE, ADAM?
WHAT DO *YOU* SEE? YOU'RE THE ONE WITH THE X-RAY VISION, MICROSCOPIC VISION, HEAT VISION, I DON'T KNOW WHAT ALL ELSE... ICE CREAM VISION? LOOK AROUND.
YOU WORKING THE ROOM? WHAT DO YOU HAVE, SON?
IT'S OKAY. ANSWER THE MAN.
NOTHING TO SHOW THE PRESENCE OF *ANYONE* IN THE ROOM BUT THE DECEASED COUNCIL MEMBER. SIR.
I'M WEARING GLOVES AND MY SUIT IS PRETTY SEALED IN, WHICH WOULD EXPLAIN ME *NOT* BEING IN EVIDENCE.
STILL, NICE *THOROUGH* JOB THE KILLER DID. CLEAN. OKAY, WHERE TO NEXT?

THEY'RE USED IN CONJUNCTION WITH THIS DEVICE.
I'VE NEVER SEEN ANYTHING LIKE THAT BEFORE.
WAIT, LET ME GUESS. ZOD. SURE, THE ARMADA WAS A NICE SURPRISE; I DON'T SEE WHY THIS SHOULD BE ANY DIFFERENT.
THAT'S THIS DEVICE'S PURPOSE...FIRING CONTAINABLE RED SUN ENERGY BURSTS INTO OVERGROWN FLORA, NOT INTO PEOPLE.
IN FACT, FIRED AT MAR-LI, WE'RE LUCKY THERE WAS SO MUCH OF HIM LEFT INTACT.
SO THIS ISN'T A MILITARY GUILD WEAPON AT ALL?
NO, IT'S A TOOL.

WE FINISHED ANALYZING THE ROOM, KAL.
YEAH, WE CHECKED, TOO. NOTHING THERE, RIGHT?
WELL...NO, NOTHING EXCEPT MAR-LI'S MATTER SPREAD AROUND... WHICH ACTUALLY DID PROVIDE US WITH A CUE.
CLUE.
CLUE. WITHIN THE BLOOD AND BODY, WE FOUND TRACES OF CARBON CASINGS FOR SMALL EXPLOSIVE ROUNDS.
NO, KAL. WE DEVELOPED THIS TO HELP WITH TERRAFORMING. THE YELLOW SUN HAS PRODUCED AREAS OF OVER-ACCELERATED PLANT GROWTH ON PARTS OF THE PLANET. FORESTS WITH IMMENSE ROOT SYSTEMS REQUIRING CONSTANT CONTROL.
LABOR GUILD.
YOU SPOKE OF MOTIVE EARLIER, KAL...HOW ADAM DIDN'T HAVE ONE. MAR-LI WAS ONE OF THE MORE ARDENT VOICES AGAINST ADMITTING A LABOR GUILD MEMBER INTO THE COUNCIL.

WE LOOKING FOR ANYONE IN PARTICULAR?

YOU'RE TELLING ME KRYPTON'S LABOR BASE HAS NO REPRESENTATION IN THE GOVERNMENT?
YES.
NO VOICE?
YES.

OF COURSE I'M NOT.
THERE'S A LOT ABOUT MY PEOPLE, MY CULTURE, THAT I DON'T LIKE.
BUT THEY'RE MY PEOPLE AND IT'S MY CULTURE, AND THE ONLY WAY TO CHANGE IT IS FROM WITHIN.

HOLD ON.

TYR-VAN?

YES, A MAN NAMED TAM-OR.
THE LABOR GUILD DOESN'T HAVE A DESIGNATED LEADER LIKE THE OTHER GUILDS, BUT HE'S BECOME SOMETHING OF THEIR SPOKESMAN IN RECENT MONTHS.

DON'T KNOW ABOUT YOU, BUT THAT'D MAKE ME PRETTY ANGRY.
ANGRY ENOUGH TO MAYBE WANT TO HURT SOMEONE.

HURTING SOMEONE AND KILLING SOMEONE ARE DIFFERENT THINGS, ADAM.
AND YOU'RE OKAY WITH THAT?

WHAT'S HAPPENED?
I'M SURPRISED YOU EVEN CARE, GENERAL EL.
IT'S JUST ANOTHER SICK MEMBER OF OUR GUILD...

...NO ONE IMPORTANT.

EVERYONE IS IMPORTANT, TYR.
NAR? I'M AT A.G. PROCESSING, SECTOR M.U. WE NEED A S.G. MEDICAL TEAM HERE RIGHT AWAY.
EN ROUTE.
IT WON'T DO ANY GOOD.
THIS HAS BEEN GOING ON FOR MONTHS NOW, AND THE SCIENCE GUILD HAS DONE NOTHING.
THE COUNCIL HAS DONE NOTHING.
ALURA ZOR-EL PROMISED TAM-OR WE WOULD GET HELP.
SHE PROMISED THE LABOR GUILD A VOICE--
--BUT IT'S ALL THE SAME, NOTHING'S CHANGED!
THE ONLY TIME ANY OF YOU COME DOWN HERE IS WHEN PRODUCTIVITY DROPS--
--WHEN YOU WANT SOMETHING FROM US!
TYR'S RIGHT.
ALURA PROMISED!
ARROGANT--
TAM-OR SAID--
--HAD ENOUGH!
LET'S GET HER INSIDE.

WHAT'S HER NAME?
SURA. SHE'S...
...SHE'S SPECIAL TO ME.
I UNDERSTAND.
YOU DIDN'T COME DOWN HERE BECAUSE WE'RE GETTING SICK, GENERAL.
NO, WE'RE LOOKING FOR TAM-OR. WE NEED TO SPEAK WITH HIM.
BECAUSE OF MAR-LI?
YOU'VE HEARD?
YOU THINK WE'RE RESPONSIBLE FOR HIS MURDER. YOU THINK TAM-OR DID IT.
I DON'T THINK ANYTHING YET. WE'RE STILL INVESTIGATING--
SUPERMAN...
...IS THAT OUR GUY?

TAM-OR--
--I NEED TO TALK TO YOU--
LEAVE HIM ALONE!
GOT HIM--
NO, WAIT--
RUN, TAM--
YOU KNOW, RUNNING JUST MAKES YOU LOOK GUILTY, BUDDY!
HOLD HIM! HOLD ON TO HIM!
NO--
GENERAL!

DON'T--
--HIT IF--
LISTEN TO ME
LET HIM GO!
ARROGANT MILITARY--
--UNH!
--KNOW WHAT YOU'RE DOING--
--WON'T LET YOU--
LISTEN TO ME--
--YOU'RE NOT HELPING.
YOU DON'T WANT TO HELP!

--AFTER TAM-OR!
LET GO OF--
THIS IS ABOUT TO TURN INTO A RIOT!
RED SHARD! PULL BACK!
YES, SIR--
UFF!
--JUST COME IN HERE AND--
NHHNFF!
--RED SHARD, WE ARE WITHDRAWING!
TYR-VAN, COME ON--
--LET'S GET YOUR FRIEND TO THE MEDICAL FACILITY.
TAKE HER WITH YOU.
I MUST STAND WITH MY GUILD.

TAM-OR! LISTEN!
THE WEAPON THAT KILLED MAR-LI, IT WAS A LABOR GUILD DEVICE--
--IF YOU DIDN'T KILL HIM, THEN SOMEONE WANTS IT TO LOOK LIKE YOU DID!
COME ON, MAN--
--WE'RE TRYING TO HELP YOU.

...HOW IS IT NONE OF YOU CAN FIND THIS GUY?
THAT'S A VERY GOOD QUESTION.
...IT'S A PLANET POPULATED BY PEOPLE WITH X-RAY VISION...
SIR?
STILL NEGATIVE REPORTS FROM THE SEARCH TEAMS.
WITH YOUR PERMISSION, I'D LIKE TO SWITCH TO THE ORBITAL SCANNERS, WE MIGHT BE ABLE TO FIND HIM THAT WAY.
THAT'S IF TAM-OR'S STILL ON PLANET.
WHERE WOULD HE GO? EARTH?
I'M GUESSING YOU HAVEN'T BEEN HOME IN A WHILE, ADAM.
EARTH ISN'T VERY FRIENDLY TO KRYPTONIANS THESE DAYS.
VERY WELL, LIEUTENANT. GO TO THE ORBITALS.
YES, SIR.

HE RAN LIKE HE WAS TERRIFIED.
OR GUILTY.

NO. I DON'T THINK HE DID IT.
NEVER MIND WHAT I THINK OF HIM AS A MAN, IT MAKES NO SENSE...

...HE WANTS NOTHING MORE THAN TO SEE THE LABOR GUILD GET THE REPRESENTATION THEY DESERVE.
MURDERING MAR-LI DOES NOTHING TO FORWARD THAT.
UNLESS HE HAD ANOTHER MOTIVE ENTIRELY.

IT'S POSSIBLE.

WE'VE BEEN LOOKING AT THIS AS A PERSONAL CRIME.
WHAT IF IT ISN'T?
WHAT DO YOU MEAN?

MAR-LI WAS A MEMBER OF THE COUNCIL, ADAM...

"...ONE OF THE LEADERS OF NEW KRYPTON.
"KILLING HIM IS A STRIKE AT THE GOVERNMENT.
"WE'VE BEEN CALLING MAR-LI'S DEATH A MURDER.
"BUT MAYBE THERE'S A DIFFERENT WORD FOR IT, ADAM...
"...MAYBE IT WAS AN ASSASSINATION..."

WORLD OF NEW KRYPTON <PART ELEVEN>
COVER ART BY **GARY FRANK** WITH **BRAD ANDERSON**

LYRA? ARE YOU EVEN LISTENING TO ME?
YES, ALURA, OF COURSE. IT WAS JUST...TODAY...HEARING ABOUT MAR-LI'S DEATH.
...AND IN SO HORRIBLE A MANNER...
FOR ANY KRYPTONIAN TO DIE IS A TRAGEDY, BUT FOR IT TO BE ONE OF THE COUNCIL...
I GUESS LIFE HAS HARDENED ME... PERHAPS TOO MUCH SO.
MY MAIN CONCERN WAS THAT WE SHOULD AUTHORIZE THE RITE OF SELECTION FOR A NEW COUNCIL MEMBER FROM THE ARTISTS GUILD.
I SHOULD REMEMBER THAT A MAN DIED.
YES, BUT YOU'RE RIGHT, I NEED TO KEEP MY MIND ON MY WORK. THESE TIMES ARE STRANGE AND WE SHOULD ALL BE ALERT.
SO LET'S--

OK, WE JUST ESCORTED ALURA TO THE COUNCIL CHAMBERS.
WHAT DO WE GOT?
HERE, SIR. THIS IS PRETTY PHYSICAL.
WE FOUND THE WEAPON.
YOU FOUND THE GUN? THAT'S... UM...
WHAT?
FORGET IT.
IT WAS LEFT DISCARDED ON A ROOFTOP TWO SPIRES OVER, HASTILY HIDDEN, EASILY FOUND.
AND YOU'RE HOLDING IT LIKE IT'S A SAILOR ON LEAVE, LADY. I HOPE YOU DUSTED IT FIRST OR SCANNED IT OR WHATEVER IT IS YOU DO.
LIEUTENANT NAR'S NO FOOL, ADAM. SHE HAS MY TRUST.
THERE YOU GO AGAIN. WHAT'S ON YOUR MIND?
TAM-OR. DESPERATE MAYBE, BUT A PRETTY SMART GUY?
GUILD LEADER. VERY SMART.
DO SMART MEN LEAVE MURDER WEAPONS "HASTILY HIDDEN AND EASILY FOUND"?

I DON'T UNDERSTAND HIM, SIR.
YEAH, I THINK HE'S BEGINNING TO ENJOY THAT. HE MEANS WHAT RESULTS, PEOPLE?
BY ANALYZING THE TRAJECTORY, GENERAL...THIS IS ABSOLUTELY WHERE THE SHOT WAS FIRED FROM.
BUT NO PHYSICAL EVIDENCE OF THE SHOOTER?
FIRST THING WE DID WAS SCAN THE WEAPON AND THE AREA AROUND IT, SIR. OF COURSE.
AND?
GENETIC RESIDUE MATCHES TAM-OR.
AND IF POOR LYRA KAM-PAR HADN'T STEPPED IN FRONT OF THE SHOT, WE'D HAVE TWO DEAD COUNCIL MEMBERS. COUNCILOR ALURA IS SO LUCKY.
RAO. IT'S CERTAINLY NOT THE FIRST TIME TAM-OR'S ACTED RADICALLY FOR THE CAUSE OF HIS GUILD, BUT--
YEAH, ASSASSINATION. DOESN'T GET ANY MORE RADICAL.
ADAM. I HAD THIS GUY RELEASED AFTER HE AND HIS MEN TOOK ALURA HOSTAGE BEFORE THIS. THESE TWO DEATHS COULD WELL BE ON MY HANDS.
AND THAT IS NOT GOOD. THAT'S...UM...

--THIS MEANS, THIS IS--
ONCE, THAT'S--THAT'S A MURDER, BUT NOW A SECOND ATTEMPT, DEAR RAO--
--MEANS WE'RE ALL IN DANGER, EVERY SINGLE ONE OF US--
WOULDN'T PUT IT PAST THEM. THEY HATE US...
YOU THINK IT'S THE HUMANS?
MAYBE YOU HAD BETTER WAIT HERE.
I WAS GOING TO SUGGEST THE SAME THING.
COUNCILORS, PLEASE--
--WE MUST REMAIN CALM!
HOW CAN YOU--OF ALL PEOPLE!--BEGIN TO ASK THAT OF US, ALURA!?
THAT SHOT WAS MEANT FOR YOU! IT'S BY THE GRACE OF RAO THAT YOU'RE STILL ALIVE!
THE SITUATION IS SPIRALING OUT OF CONTROL. WE MUST ACT...
...AND WE MUST ACT DECISIVELY. IF IT IS THE LABOR GUILD THAT'S RESPONSIBLE FOR THIS, RATHER THAN THE HUMANS--
THAT IS ONLY A THEORY, COUNCILOR ZO, ONE OF SEVERAL--

IT MAY BE MORE THAN THAT, AUNT ALURA.
...WE LOCATED AND ANALYZED THE WEAPON THAT KILLED LYRA KAM-PAR. THERE WAS GENETIC RESIDUE LEFT ON THE RIFLE.
IT'S A CLEAN MATCH TO TAM-OR.

NOT TAM-OR... I NEVER THOUGHT--
PLEASE TELL US YOU'VE ARRESTED HIM, GENERAL EL.

WE CAN'T FIND HIM, COUNCILOR ZO.
IS IT POSSIBLE HE FLED THE PLANET? THE WAY RAL-DAR DID, WHEN HE TRIED TO ASSASSINATE GENERAL ZOD?
I CHECKED WITH THE DEFENSE GRID BEFORE COMING HERE.
ORBITAL SENSORS CONFIRM THAT NO ONE HAS LEFT THE PLANET SINCE MAR-LI'S MURDER.

THEN TAM-OR IS STILL ON-PLANET.
THAT'S HOW IT APPEARS, YES.
HE'LL COME AFTER ONE OF US NEXT.
NONE OF US ARE SAFE.

A PLANET FULL OF MEN AND WOMEN WHO CAN SEE THROUGH SOLID STONE...
...AND YET HE MANAGES TO EVADE YOU, GENERAL EL?
HE'S EITHER VERY SCARED OR VERY SMART.

OR HE IS BEING HELPED.
MUCH AS WE SUSPECTED RAL-DAR WAS HELPED.
THE LABOR GUILD, THEY MUST BE SHIELDING HIM. THEY ALWAYS PROTECT THEIR OWN.
THERE WAS ALMOST A RIOT WHEN YOU TRIED TO ARREST HIM IN THE AGRO SECTOR.
THAT WAS BAD TIMING AS MUCH AS ANYTHING.
THE LABOR GUILD DOESN'T HAVE MUCH REASON TO TRUST US RIGHT NOW.
WHY WOULDN'T THEY? WE HAVE ALWAYS DEFENDED THEM, ALWAYS CARED FOR THEM--
THEY'RE PEOPLE, NOT PETS, COUNCILOR ZO.
PEOPLE WHO ARE BEING DEVASTATED BY AN ILLNESS THAT SEEMS TO TARGET ONLY THEM, IN FACT.
IS IT ANY WONDER THEY RESENTED MY ARRIVAL? COMING TO TAKE THEIR LEADER INSTEAD OF OFFERING ANY HELP, ANY AID?
WE ARE TRYING TO HELP! I'VE BEEN TREATING THE WORKERS FOR MONTHS--
I HAVE TO WONDER HOW SERIOUSLY YOU'RE PURSUING TAM-OR, GENERAL.
WHAT DID YOU SAY, COUNCILOR?
YOUR MOTHER WAS LABOR GUILD, WASN'T SHE? A JUMP-UP...
...ELEVATED TO SCIENCE GUILD WHEN JOR-EL MARRIED HER, ISN'T THAT RIGHT?
"ELEVATED"?
THIS IS GETTING US NOWHERE.

I SUGGEST SENDING TROOPS INTO THE LABOR GUILD SECTOR, TO KEEP AN EYE ON THEM, AT LEAST UNTIL TAM-OR IS CAUGHT.
JUST TO BE ON THE SAFE SIDE.
I AGREE--
ARE YOU BOTH SUNTOUCHED?
KAL AVOIDED A RIOT, YOU WANT TO START ONE.
WITHOUT THE LABOR GUILD, OUR SOCIETY WILL COLLAPSE, COUNCILORS.
DO NOT MISTAKE THE ACTIONS OF ONE MAN FOR HIS GUILD.
WE DID NOT BLAME THE MILITARY GUILD FOR RAL-DAR, KAY-ZO.
HEAR HER!
I CONCUR.
I'M DOUBLING THE GUARD ON ALL THE COUNCIL MEMBERS.
HALF THE MILITARY GUILD IS OUT LOOKING FOR TAM-OR.
WE WILL FIND HIM.
I CERTAINLY HOPE YOU DO.
FOR ALL OUR SAKES, GENERAL...
...INCLUDING YOURS.

WHERE ARE WE HEADING?
THE MEDICAL FACILITY.

WENT THAT WELL, DID IT?
THEY'RE FRIGHTENED, THEY BELIEVE THEY'RE BEING HUNTED.
I'M TRYING TO REMIND MYSELF OF THAT.

DO YOU REALLY THINK THIS TAM-OR GUY DID IT?
IT CERTAINLY LOOKS THAT WAY.

I JUST DON'T KNOW.

WHO ARE WE LOOKING FOR?
TYR-VAN. HE'S LABOR GUILD.
THE ONE WITH THE SICK GIRLFRIEND, RIGHT...
...YOU THINK HE MIGHT BE ABLE TO HELP?
PERHAPS...
...SEE IF YOU CAN FIND HIM, I'LL CATCH UP...
...I NEED TO TALK TO SOMEONE FIRST.

GENERAL NHH EL...
...A HNGG PLEASANT SURPRISE.

HOW ARE YOU FEELING, GENERAL ZOD?
MUCH GNFF BETTER, THANK YOU.
THOUGH THE MUSCLE RETRAINING GNHHH IS NFFF TEDIOUS.

I HEARD ABOUT COUNCILOR MAR-LI.
SOMEONE MADE AN ATTEMPT ON ALURA THIS MORNING.
HER ASSISTANT, LYRA KAM-PAR, WAS KILLED BY ACCIDENT.

YES, URSA TELLS ME THAT TAM-OR IS THE PRIME SUSPECT.

RIGHT NOW, HE'S THE ONLY SUSPECT.
THE SAME TAM-OR WHO TOOK ALURA HOSTAGE?
UNLESS THERE'S ANOTHER ONE.

HE'S INNOCENT.

WE FOUND HIS D.N.A. ON THE RIFLE THAT KILLED KAM-PAR.
KAL-EL, YOU STILL THINK LIKE A HUMAN.

DO YOU REALLY IMAGINE IT WOULD BE DIFFICULT FOR A KRYPTONIAN-- WITH OUR POWERS, WITH OUR TECH-NOLOGY--
--TO PLANT GENETIC MATERIAL?

TAM-OR NEARLY GOT HIMSELF AND HIS FOLLOWERS KILLED WHEN HE TOOK ALURA HOSTAGE. THE MAN IS SMART, YES, BUT HE'S NOT A TACTICIAN.
NOW THE SAME MAN MANAGES TO MURDER MAR-LI FROM WITHIN A LOCKED ROOM...
...BUT MISSES HIS TARGET WHEN SHOOTING AT ALURA?

CAN'T HAVE IT BOTH WAYS, YOU'RE SAYING?
EITHER HE'S A BRILLIANT TACTICIAN OR HE'S NOT.

HE'S NOT. HE'S AN IDEALIST.
AND THEY RARELY MAKE GOOD GENERALS.
YOU'RE LOOKING FOR THE WRONG MAN.

BUT MAYBE HE CAN LEAD ME TO THE RIGHT ONE.

YOU WERE RIGHT TO LET ME HANDLE THIS, ADAM.
WRI-QIN, I THOUGHT YOU'D STILL BE DEBATING IN THE COUNCIL CHAMBER.
DEBATING? ARGUING AND POSTURING ARE BETTER WORDS TO DESCRIBE IT.
AND FAR LESS USEFUL THAN THE WORK I CAN DO HERE. IS THERE SOMETHING I CAN HELP YOU WITH?
"...IT ISN'T YOU WE'RE HERE TO SEE."
TYR-VAN.
TYR?
HOW DID THIS ALL GET SO WRONG? WHY DIDN'T YOU DO SOMETHING?
YES, I BETRAYED YOU, YES. BUT I TRUSTED YOU, CRAZY AS THAT SOUNDS. YOU SAID YOU'D HELP THE LABOR GUILD. HOW DID YOU LET ALL THIS HAPPEN?
PEOPLE ARE SICK, GENERAL.
NO, NOT JUST SICK...PEOPLE ARE DEAD. MOST NOTABLY COUNCILOR MAR-LI. MURDERED. AND TAM-OR IS GUILTY IN EVERYONE'S EYES.

IT'S THE INVESTIGATION. WE'RE--
INVESTIGATING.
THEN AGAIN I ASK, HOW CAN I HELP? OR...AM I IN DANGER?
NOT TO OUR KNOWLEDGE. I'M GLAD YOU'RE GUARDED, I WON'T LIE, BUT NO, THAT'S NOT WHY WE'RE HERE.
IN FACT...
WHAT?
I'M SORRY YOUR FRIEND IS SICK.
FRIEND? I LOVE SURA, IF YOU MUST KNOW. AND "SORRY" DOESN'T MAKE HER WELL, DOES IT, GENERAL?
"SORRY" DOESN'T MAKE THINGS RIGHT.
IT STRIKES ME THAT THINGS ARE WORSE FOR US NOW THAN THEY WERE BEFORE YOU CAME.

YEAH, I DESERVE THAT, I GUESS.
BUT I'M HERE TO SEE YOU NOW FOR PRECISELY THAT REASON, TYR. WE'RE NOT SURE TAM-OR IS GUILTY AT ALL.
THINGS ARE ADDING UP TO SAY HE IS, SURE, BUT MAYBE THEY'RE ADDING UP A BIT TOO EASILY.
WE NEED TO SPEAK TO HIM, TYR.
I KNOW A PLACE.

SO YOU'RE FROM EARTH?
USED TO BE. BUT IT WAS CERTAINLY AS A MAN OF RANN THAT I CAME HERE TO PROTEST NEW KRYPTON'S CHARTER WITH THANAGAR.
I ENVY YOU THE STARS, ADAM.
OH, I HAVE SEEN SOME WONDERFUL THINGS, TYR.
BUT OUT IN SPACE, I'VE ALSO SEEN PAIN AND TERROR.
I'M WARILY WAITING TO SEE WHICH I ENCOUNTER MORE WITH MY NEW TEAM ...PAIN OR WONDER. WITH VRIL DOX AROUND, I HAVE MY FEARS...
HERE WE ARE.

OH, MAN. THIS IS PRETTY.
TYR? WHERE IN RAO'S NAME ARE WE?!
ZOD.
GE--RAL! NEWS-- Z--GEN--AL--
NAR!
WALLS MUST BE LEAD-LINED OR--
TYR? PLEASE... WHAT IS THIS PLACE?
MILITARY TEAMS HAVE BEEN BRINGING THESE ALIENS IN FOR MONTHS NOW.
THE LABOR GUILD... WE BUILT THIS PLACE...LEAD-LINED WALLS LIKE YOU JUST SAID...PLUS SOUNDPROOFED TO EVEN THE DECIBEL RANGE OF OUR EARS.
AND ON ARMY ORDERS WE KILL THE CREATURES, TOO.

HOW CAN YOU NOT KNOW, KAL? THIS IS MILITARY. THIS IS ZOD. IF YOU'RE TRULY THE HEAD OF THE ARMY, HOW IS THIS A SURPRISE?
WHY? WHY THE BUTCHERY?
THEIR HIDES. DON'T ASK ME WHY.
SOME GO TO THE SCIENCE GUILD ALIVE. SOME JUST THEIR SILVER SKINS.
AGAIN KAL, HOW CAN YOU NOT KNOW THIS?
COME ON. LET'S FIND TAM-OR.

TYR!
WHAT ARE THEY DOING HERE? WHY DID YOU LEAD THEM HERE?!?
IT'S NOT WHAT YOU THINK, TAM!
THEY WANT TO HELP YOU!
HELP? THE WAY THEY HELPED YESTERDAY?
I DIDN'T KILL THE COUNCILOR! I DIDN'T DO ANYTHING!
YOU RAN.
BECAUSE YOU WERE GOING TO KILL ME!
WHY WOULD YOU THINK THAT?
I KNOW WHO MY FRIENDS ARE!
HE WARNED ME YOU WERE COMING.
WHO-EVER YOUR FRIEND IS, HE LIED TO YOU.
HELP US CLEAR YOUR NAME, TAM.
HELP US CLEAR THE LABOR GUILD'S NAME.
RAO HELP ME.
GENERAL EL--

--EXCELLENT WORK. WE'LL TAKE IT FROM HERE.
COUNCILOR ZO! YOU HAD US FOLLOWED?
TRACKED, GENERAL. COMMANDER GOR'S IDEA.
THERE WAS SOME QUESTION ABOUT YOUR LOYALTIES, AS I SAID.
THIS MAN IS INNOCENT, COUNCILOR.
MOVE OUT OF THE WAY, GENERAL...
...OR I WILL ARREST YOU FOR AIDING AND ABETTING.
ON WHOSE AUTHORITY? I COMMAND THE MILITARY GUILD, I--
DIDN'T NAR GIVE YOU THE NEWS, EL...
...AS OF TWELVE MINUTES AGO, GENERAL ZOD RETURNED TO ACTIVE DUTY.
YOU'VE BEEN DEMOTED.
AND GENERAL ZOD'S POLICY TOWARDS TRAITORS IS VERY CLEAR--

--THEY'RE TO BE EXECUTED ON SIGHT!
RED SUN OFF! SWITCH TO KINETICS!
READY... ...AIM...
...FIRE!

WORLD OF NEW KRYPTON <PART TWELVE>
COVER ART BY **GARY FRANK** WITH **BRAD ANDERSON**

FIRE!
IS THIS HOW IT IS FOR SUPERMAN? (...CAN'T BRING MYSELF TO CALL HIM COMMANDER EL.)
IS THIS HOW IT IS ALL THE TIME?
HE CAN MOVE AT THE SPEED OF...LIGHT? SOUND?
DUNNO, BUT FAST... SUPER FAST.
DOES HE ALWAYS SEE THINGS SLOWED DOWN...PEOPLE, THINGS, MOVING LIKE SNAILS?
I'LL HAVE TO ASK HIM IF WE LIVE.
I SEE THE BLASTS FIRED. TIME SLOWS DOWN IN THESE MOMENTS...LIFE AND DEATH. SURE.
I SEE THEM COMING.
WHY ARE THEY SO SLOW?
MY FINGERS MOVE LIKE MERCURY ON GLASS. I TOUCH THE BUTTON ON MY BUCKLE, AND...

...WE SAY GOODBYE TO ALL OF THIS.
AD--
--AM!

WHAT DID YOU DO?
SAVED US. ZETAED US OUT AND BACK... WHIPLASH PROGRAM...
GOD KNOWS WHERE WE ARE, THOUGH. TOLD YOU ZETA BEAMS WEREN'T PRECISE.
IT'S KRYPTON, AND WE'RE OUT OF DANGER--THAT'S GOOD ENOUGH.
HEY, CLARK.
YEAH?

YOUR PLANET SURE IS BEAUTIFUL.
I AGREE, EARTHMAN. COMMANDER EL. THANK YOU FOR THIS...
IF...I'M TO D...DIE...BETTER HERE THAN...THAT... SLAUGHTER-HOUSE.
WHAT'RE YOU TALKING ABOUT, TAM-OR? NO ONE'S GOING TO DIE.
I B... BEG TO... DIFFER.
YOU WERE FAST, YES...
I W...WANTED TO SAVE MY PEOPLE...ALL ANY OF US... WANTED.
AND... WE...WERE... FOOLS.
COMMANDER EL! ADAM STRANGE OF EARTH!
YOU ARE UNDER ARREST FOR TREASONOUS AND UNLAWFUL ACTIONS.

...BUT SO ARE SPEEDING BULLETS.
TAM! NO!
ADAM, HELP ME!
THE RED SUN BEAM THEY FIRED...MY POWERS ARE DOWN--
RRRIP
S'CHEST WOUND, KAL! HEART, OR CLOSE TO. THERE'S NO TIME--
THERE'S TIME! WE CAN GET HIM TO DOCTORS... MEDICS CAN--
NO, COMMANDER...NO DOCTOR...
AND BY MY COUNT, YOU'RE JUST SHY TWENTY MORE MINUTES UNDER RED SUN EFFECT...

...SO PLEASE, EL, I BEG YOU...
...RESIST.
YOU JUST MURDERED AN INNOCENT MAN.
YOU THINK BECAUSE I DON'T HAVE MY POWERS RIGHT NOW, I'M NO THREAT TO YOU?
GOR...
...I'M MORE DANGEROUS RIGHT NOW THAN EVER.
...LET'S TEST THA--
STAND DOWN!

BY RAO'S BREATH, WHAT HAPPENED HERE?!
WHO'S RESPONSIBLE FOR THIS?
COMMANDER GOR! AN ANSWER!
SIR! TH-THE FUGITIVES ATTEMPTED TO ESCAPE--
SHUT UP.
MY ORDERS WERE NO LETHAL FORCE.
IF YOU CANNOT FOLLOW ORDERS, YOU HAVE NO BUSINESS GIVING THEM.
YOU'RE HEREBY DEMOTED TO LANCEPE-SADE--
GENERAL!
COMMANDER GOR WAS ACTING ON MY AUTHORITY, ON COUNCIL AUTHORITY--
THEN LANCEPESADE GOR SHOULD HAVE RESIGNED. BUT WHILE HE IS IN UNIFORM, HE DOES WHAT I SAY, NOT WHAT THE COUNCIL SAYS.
AND WHILE I CEDED MY SEAT ON THE COUNCIL TO YOU, YOU DID NOT GET LEADERSHIP OF THE MILITARY GUILD WITH IT.
MY GUILD, COUNCILOR ZO.
MY ORDERS.
CLEAR?

GO AWAY.
URSA, TAKE TAM-OR'S BODY TO MEDICAL, WITH RESPECT.
YOU'RE ALL DISMISSED.
WE'LL SAVE YOUR INEVITABLE QUESTIONS ABOUT THE RESEARCH FACILITY FOR LATER, COMMANDER EL, IF YOU DON'T MIND.
BUT THEY WILL BE ANSWERED.
CERTAINLY. FOR NOW, HOWEVER...
...I WOULD ASK YOUR FRIEND TO LEAVE.
WHILE I HAVE NO DOUBT YOUR ASSISTANCE HAS BEEN INVALUABLE, ADAM STRANGE, COUNCILOR ZO'S ACTIONS--IF NOT THE NATURE OF THE ASSASSINATIONS--HAS TURNED THE SITUATION INTO A POLITICAL ONE.
I'M NOT SURE I UNDERSTAND, GENERAL...ZOD, IS IT?
HE'S REFERRING TO YOUR STATUS AS A REPRESENTATIVE OF RANN.
THIS IS A SENSITIVE INTERNAL MATTER. I'M SURE YOU UNDERSTAND.

KAL?
IT'S ALL RIGHT, ADAM.
THANKS FOR EVERYTHING...
...AND SAFE TRAVELS.
WAS TAM-OR ABLE TO GIVE YOU ANYTHING USEFUL BEFORE HE DIED?
JUST THAT HE WAS BEING MANIPULATED.
HE KNEW WHO WAS RESPONSIBLE, BUT HE DIED BEFORE HE COULD TELL US.
SO WHERE DOES THAT LEAVE YOUR INVESTIGATION?
IT LEAVES US, GENERAL...

"...BACK WHERE WE STARTED."
FROM THE BEGINNING, THEN...
...URSA RELAYED WHAT SHE COULD OF THE INVESTIGATION TO ME, BUT I AM CERTAIN THERE ARE THINGS I AM MISSING.
LET'S GO THROUGH IT AGAIN.
FIRST VICTIM...
...COUNCILOR MAR-LI OF THE ARTISTS GUILD. FOUND MURDERED IN HIS ROOMS, THE SECURITY SYSTEMS ALL ACTIVATED. NO SIGNS OF HOW THE KILLER GOT IN OR OUT.
WEAPON USED WAS A LABOR GUILD FRAGMENTATION DRILL.
SECOND VICTIM, LYRA KAMPAR, ASSISTANT TO ALURA ZOR-EL.
SHOT WITH A TWO-STAGE VANGUARD SNIPER'S RIFLE, MILITARY GUILD ISSUE.
THE SHOT WAS MEANT FOR COUNCILOR ALURA.

BUT IF THE SHOT WASN'T MEANT FOR ALURA? BUT FOR KAM-PAR, INSTEAD?
I CONSIDERED THAT. THERE'S NOTHING TO LINK KAM-PAR AND MAR-LI THAT WE'VE FOUND.
THAT FACILITY, WHERE WE FOUND TAM-OR. COULD IT BE THE LINK?
OR EVEN THE SOURCE OF THE ILLNESS THAT'S DEVASTATING THE LABOR GUILD?
WHATEVER HAS STRUCK DOWN THE LABOR GUILD, IT DOESN'T COME FROM THERE. I MADE CERTAIN OF THAT.
AS FOR THE LOCATION AS MOTIVE, NEITHER MAR-LI NOR KAM-PAR HAD KNOWLEDGE OF THE BASE. I WAS KEEPING IT SECRET FOR A REASON.
BECAUSE YOU'RE PREPARING FOR WAR.
NO, KAL-EL. I AM PREPARING TO DEFEND AGAINST ONE.
THEN WHY THE SECRECY?
YOU'VE BEEN HERE LONG ENOUGH TO KNOW THAT ANSWER.
NEW KRYPTON LIVES WITH THE MEMORY OF BRAINIAC. CAUTION TURNS TO FEAR TURNS TO PANIC QUICKLY AMONG THEM.
I SEE. AND NOT BECAUSE YOU'RE VIVISECTING ALIENS FOR PARTS THERE?
THAT RESEARCH GOES DIRECTLY TO DEFENSE.
IT GOES TO ENSURING THE SURVIVAL OF OUR PEOPLE.
"OUR PEOPLE."

WHAT?
THAT'S WHAT TAM-OR SAID, TOO. AND SOMEONE ELSE.
RAL-DAR...
I'M DOING THIS TO SAVE OUR PEOPLE.
RAL-DAR WAS AS LOYAL AND DEDICATED TO NEW KRYPTON AS ANY MAN.
I STILL FIND HIS BETRAYAL IMPOSSIBLE TO ACCEPT.
MAYBE IT WASN'T BETRAYAL.
MAYBE HE WAS MISLED.
MAYBE THEY ALL WERE.

EXPLAIN YOURSELF, COMMANDER.
RAL-DAR THOUGHT HE WAS PROTECTING NEW KRYPTON WHEN HE SHOT YOU. HE THOUGHT YOU WOULD START A WAR.
BUT HIS ACTIONS ON EARTH WERE MANIPULATED TO RAISE TENSIONS EVEN HIGHER.
USED BY GENERAL LANE TO REVEAL AND PROMOTE HIMSELF.
YOU'RE SAYING SOMEONE ON NEW KRYPTON IS MANIPULATING OUR OWN PEOPLE IN SUPPORT OF EARTH?
PERHAPS. THERE'S GOT TO BE A LINK, SOMEONE, SOMETHING, THAT TIES ALL OF THIS TOGETHER.
TAM-OR SAID HE'D BEEN TRICKED. "TRICKED US," IN FACT.
THIS...CABAL YOU'RE IMAGINING, THEY'VE DONE THE OPPOSITE.
INSTEAD OF STRENGTHENING US, THE FOOLS HAVE WEAKENED US.
YOU SAID YOU MADE CERTAIN THE LABOR GUILD ILLNESS WASN'T THE RESULT OF THE WORK AT THAT BASE. HOW?
I WAS COORDINATING RESEARCH WITH THE SCIENCE GUILD.
NOT ALURA?
NO, SHE'S... FAR TOO SQUEAMISH FOR THAT KIND OF THING.
COUNCILOR WRI-QIN.
NOW I'M THE FOOL.
I THOUGHT TAM-OR WAS SAYING "NO DOCTOR" AS HE DIED. THAT IT WAS TOO LATE TO SAVE HIM.
THAT WASN'T WHAT HE WAS SAYING AT ALL.

ISN'T THE VIEW BREATHTAKING?
NOT REALLY JEWELS, OBVIOUSLY.
YEAH, ORE OF A CERTAIN KIND THAT, WHEN LIGHT IS SHONE THROUGH, GIVES IT THAT EFFECT. I KNOW MY HOMEWORLD.
AND THAT SAME ORE, WHEN COMBINED WITH BOTH LIGHT AND WATER, MAKES THAT WATER...OR WATERFALL IN THIS INSTANCE...SEEM FIERY RED.
I'M SO GLAD I HAD A RETREAT BUILT HERE. IT REALLY DOES REMIND ME OF A MUCH HAPPIER TIME.
A HAPPIER LIFE. ON KRYPTON. WHEN I GAZE OUT, THAT'S WHAT I SEE.
HUH. I GUESSED YOU'D WORKED IT OUT WHEN YOU ASKED TO SEE ME HERE.
INDEED!

I REMEMBER SEEING THE ORIGINAL VERSION OF THIS ON KRYPTON AS A BOY.
THE JEWEL MOUNTAINS.
AND WHAT I SEE... IS A PRIVILEGED GUY WHO ALREADY HAS A GOOD LIFE. A BEAUTIFUL HOME. SEAT ON THE COUNCIL. BUT IT'S STILL NOT ENOUGH, EH, WRI-QIN?
I'VE MET YOUR KIND ON EARTH.
MY HOME IS FITTED WITH... "INSURANCE" AGAINST THE EVENTUALITY OF SOMETHING LIKE THIS.
YOU'VE BEEN BOMBARDED WITH A CONCENTRATED BEAM OF SUNSTONE CRYSTAL THAT'S AKIN TO SYNTHESIZED GOLD KRYPTONITE.

WHAT *IS* IT THEY CALL YOU ON EARTH? SUPERMAN? WELL *NOT* TODAY.
TODAY THAT'S *ME.*

WHY, WRI-QIN? THE MURDERS. AT LEAST TELL--
WHY? WAR. *WAR IS COMING.*
EARTH?

"THE FEMALE FROM EARTH. SHE BRIEFLY LIVED HERE AMONG US IN THE GUISE OF *SUPERWOMAN.*

MAKE NEW KRYPTON MORE *EASILY DEFEATABLE.*

BUT *WHY* WOULD YOU *POSSIBLY* WANT THAT?

A *QUICKER* VICTORY FOR EARTH. LANE SAID THAT *IF* HE GOT THAT...HE'D SPARE OUR PLANET. *THAT'S* WHY SOME OF THE CABAL ACTED...

...THEY WANTED TO SAVE THEIR PEOPLE. *ME,* I COULDN'T CARE LESS.

OF COURSE WITH EARTH. OF COURSE. GENERAL LANE, HE'S BEEN READYING EARTH SINCE EVEN BEFORE WE CAME OUT OF BRAINIAC'S BOTTLE.
ONCE WE WERE OUT, SHE CAME ON HIS BEHALF TO RECRUIT US.
"SHE CONVINCED US TO WEAKEN KRYPTON. TO RELAY INFORMATION. FOSTER ILLNESS IN THE WORKPLACE AND DISCORD ON THE STREETS.
"EACH OF US WAS IN A POSITION WHERE WE COULD ACCOMPLISH AT LEAST ONE OF THESE GOALS."
YOU SAID IT YOURSELF. I'M PRIVILEGED AND GREEDY.
LANE SAID THERE'D BE POSITIONS OF POWER FOR US WITHIN THE GOVERNMENT OF A KRYPTON RULED BY EARTH.
BUT THEN I GOT TO THINKING...WHY SHARE? MY FELLOW CONSPIRATORS HAD DONE WHAT WAS ASKED OF THEM.
THEY'D SERVED THEIR PURPOSE. I WANTED THEIR SHARE OF THE SPOILS. SIMPLE.

YES, PITY IT DIDN'T WORK OUT.
I WONDER WHAT LIFE ON EARTH WILL BE LIKE... ME WITH POWERS AND EVERYONE ELSE LIKE YOU ARE NOW.
WRI-QIN...DO YOU...CHOK...THINK I'M...STUPID?

YOU THINK LANE'S GOING TO ROLL OUT THE "WELCOME MAT"? YOU SHOULD TALK TO RAL-DAR ABOUT THAT.
OH WAIT, HE'S **DEAD.**
'SIDES, YOU'RE **NOT** GOING ANYWHERE.
AND **HOW** ARE YOU GOING TO STOP ME?
NAR. RED SHARD. MOVE IN.
IN.

COMMANDER?
WRI-QIN'S IN SECURE HOLDING.
THE COUNCIL IS ABOUT TO MEET. GENERAL ZOD HAS ASKED FOR YOUR PRESENCE.
THANK YOU, LIEUTENANT NAR.
NORMALLY, WHEN I GIVE A SUMMONS...
...PEOPLE JUMP TO OBEY IT.
IS THERE A REASON YOU NEGLECTED TO JOIN US?
I DIDN'T SEE MUCH POINT IN IT.

YOU WERE MISTAKEN. THE COUNCILORS GRANTED THE LABOR GUILD A SEAT ON THE COUNCIL.
YOUR FRIEND TYR-VAN HAS BEEN NAMED THE HEAD OF THE GUILD.
HE WILL WANT TO THANK YOU FOR WHAT YOU'VE DONE.
I'VE BEEN THINKING ABOUT THAT...
...IT SEEMS I'VE BEEN HERE FOREVER, AND I CAN'T SEE THE DIFFERENCE I'VE MADE.
YOU WERE JUST INSTRUMENTAL IN CHANGING THE FOUNDATION OF OUR SOCIETY.
IF THAT DOES NOT SATISFY YOU, YOUR EGO IS EVEN LARGER THAN MINE, EL.
I'M A MAN OF TWO WORLDS, GENERAL, STILL TRYING TO FIGURE OUT HOW TO SERVE EACH OF THEM.
THAT WRI-QIN COULD BETRAY SO MANY...I HAD WANTED MY PEOPLE TO BE BETTER THAN THAT.
THAT WAS, PERHAPS, NAIVE OF YOU.
I'D RATHER SAY HOPEFUL.
SPEAKING AS YOUR ADVERSARY, EVEN AS, AT TIMES, YOUR ENEMY, YOU HAVE CHANGED NEW KRYPTON FOR THE BETTER.
COMING FROM YOU, I'LL TAKE THAT AS A COMPLIMENT.
I COULDN'T CARE LESS HOW YOU TAKE IT.
I JUST WANT NEW KRYPTON TO SURVIVE.
TO SEE MY PEOPLE HAVE A SECOND CHANCE--
YOU WERE TALKING ABOUT SECOND CHANCES, KAL-EL...

...WE MAY HAVE JUST LOST OURS....
THE END?

SUPERMAN: WORLD OF NEW KRYPTON #6
<VARIANT COVER BY EDDY BARROWS & RUY JOSÉ WITH ROD REIS>

SUPERMAN: WORLD OF NEW KRYPTON #7
<VARIANT COVER BY BRYAN TALBOT>

SUPERMAN: WORLD OF NEW KRYPTON #8
<VARIANT COVER BY JOE KUBERT WITH PETE CARLSSON>

SUPERMAN: WORLD OF NEW KRYPTON #9
<VARIANT COVER BY MARK BUCKINGHAM WITH BRAD ANDERSON>

SUPERMAN: WORLD OF NEW KRYPTON #10
<VARIANT COVER BY DUSTIN NGUYEN>

SUPERMAN: WORLD OF NEW KRYPTON #11 <VARIANT COVER BY VICTOR IBAÑEZ>

SUPERMAN: WORLD OF NEW KRYPTON #12
<VARIANT COVER BY LADRÖNN>

WORLD OF NEW KRYPTON
<SKETCH GALLERY>

<FOLLOWING FIVE PAGES>
A deleted scene originally intended for SUPERMAN: WORLD OF NEW KRYPTON #1. After Pete Woods drew these five pages, the story was reworked and the pages cut.

<NEW KRYPTON DESIGNS>
Sketches and 3-D modeling by Pete Woods

<NEW KRYPTON INTERIORS>

Sketches and 3-D modeling by Pete Woods

<THE BRIEFING ROOM>

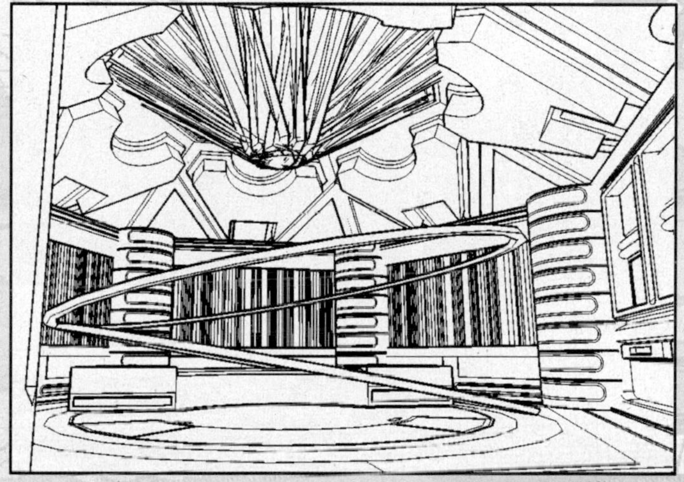

<PRISON UNIT>

<THE TRIAL CHAMBER>

<THANAGARIANS>

Designs by Pete Woods

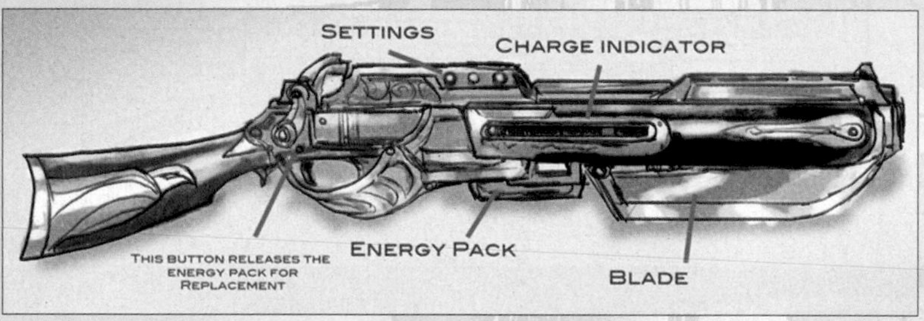

<KAL-EL'S GUILD UNIFORMS>

Designs by Gary Frank

Originally, the plan was for Kal-El to join New Krypton's Labor Guild (top left, and bottom). But ultimately it was decided that he would join the Military Guild (top right) so as to better play up the drama between him and Zod.

<COVER SKETCHES

<DUSTIN NGUYEN

<ERIC CANETE

<VICTOR IBAÑEZ>

<GARY FRANK>

<JOE KUBERT>

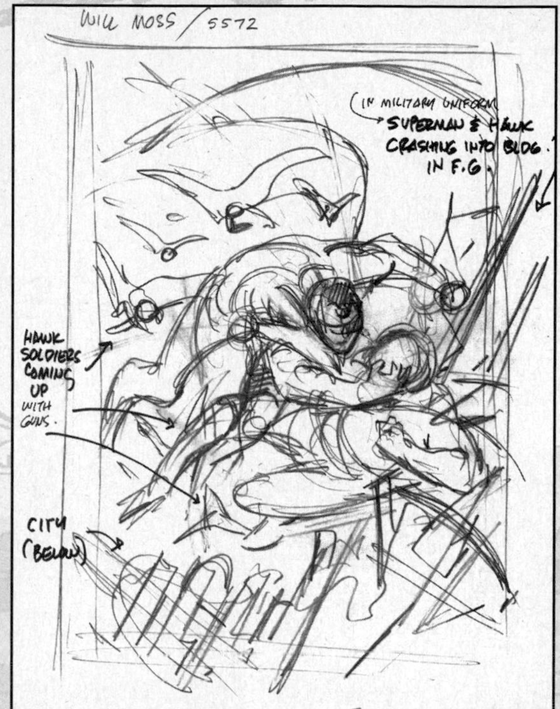

<MARK BUCKINGHAM>

<ZOR-EL'S TOMB>
3-D modeling by Pete Woods

<ALURA'S COSTUMES & KRYPTONIAN ASSAULT RIFLE>

Art by Pete Woods

A
B
C

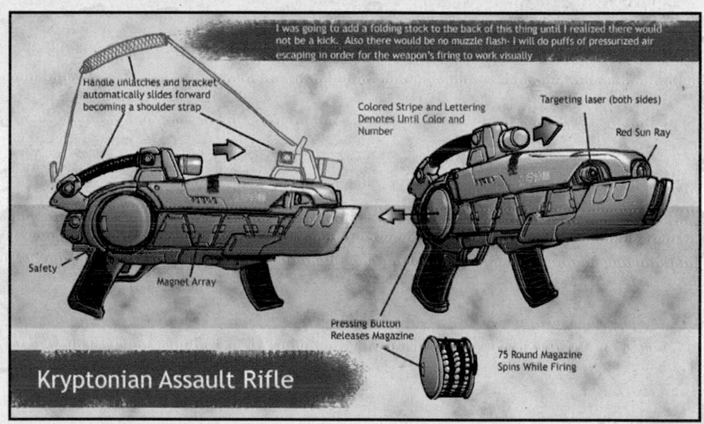
I was going to add a folding stock to the back of this thing until I realized there would not be a kick. Also there would be no muzzle flash- I will do puffs of pressurized air escaping in order for the weapon's firing to work visually
Handle unlatches and bracket automatically slides forward becoming a shoulder strap
Colored Stripe and Lettering Denotes Until Color and Number
Targeting laser (both sides)
Red Sun Ray
Safety
Magnet Array
Pressing Button Releases Magazine
75 Round Magazine Spins While Firing
Kryptonian Assault Rifle

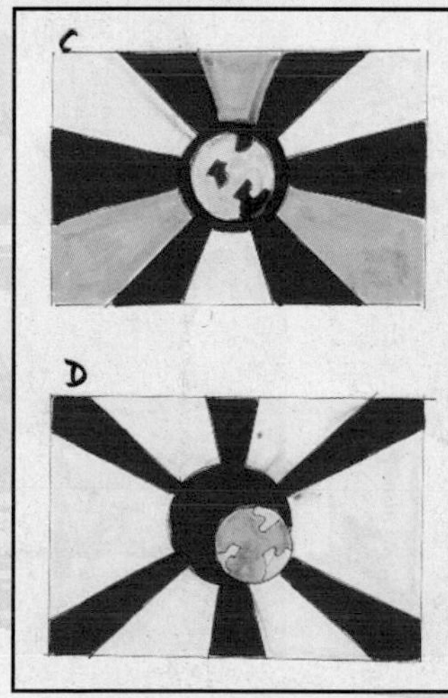
C
D

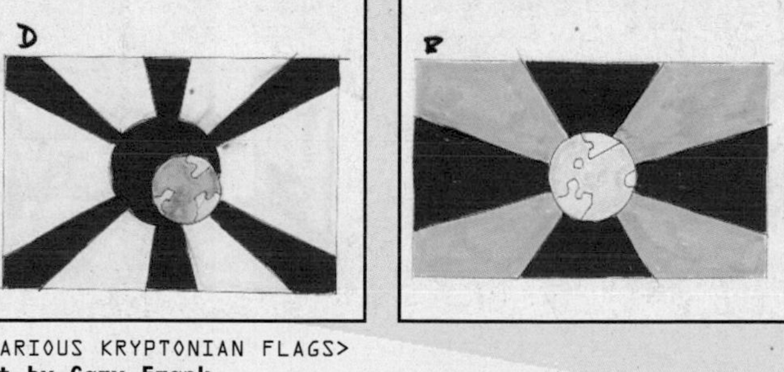
A
B

<VARIOUS KRYPTONIAN FLAGS>
Art by Gary Frank

All art by Pete Woods

<JEMM, SON OF SATURN>

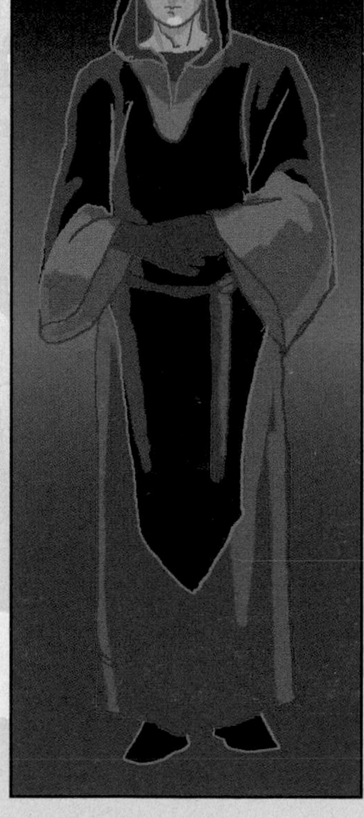

<RELIGIOUS GUILD>